CONSULT THE ORACLE

ORACLE

A Victorian Guide to Folklore and Fortune Telling

Published in Great Britain in 2013 by Old House books & maps, Midland House, West Way, Botley, Oxford OX2 0PH, United Kingdom.
4301 21st Street, Suite 220B, Long Island City, NY 11101, USA.
Website: www.oldhousebooks.co.uk

A CIP catalogue record for this book is available from the British Library.

This is an abridged version of a book originally published in 1899 by C. A. Pearson Ltd, London.

ISBN-13: 978 1 90840 273 8

Illustrations are acknowledged as follows:
Mary Evans Picture Library, cover image (detail), pages 31, 81, 89, 92, 93, 96 and 131.

Edited by Fern Riddell.

Printed in China through Worldprint Ltd.
13 14 15 16 17 10 9 8 7 6 5 4 3 2 1

CONSULT THE ORACLE

A Victorian Guide to Folklore and Fortune Telling

GABRIEL NOSTRADAMUS

1899

CONTENTS

CHAPTER ONE

EVERYDAY
SUPERSTITIONS

THINGS TO REMEMBER

WELL-SPOKEN OF AND ILL-SPOKEN OF

THE left cheek is the "friend cheek." When you hear a singing in your left ear there is someone speaking well of you; if the singing is in the other ear it is someone speaking ill. In the latter case *bite your little finger very hard*, and the person talking ill of you will bite his or her tongue just as hard.

If you have your clothes mended upon your back you will be ill-spoken of.

AGAINST EVIL SPIRITS

When opening the window at night always make the sign of the cross with the forefinger against the glass. It is a sure method of preventing the evil spirits who hover about in the dark from seizing the opportunity to enter the house.

IT IS DANGEROUS TO WEAR YELLOW AND GREEN

Yellow is the colour of jealousy. Green is also a colour of jealousy and of fickleness as well. "Green, forsaken clean," says the proverb. A well-known rhyme has it –

"Green's forsaken,
  And yellow's forsworn,
  And blue's the sweetest
  Colour that's worn."

One of Dr. Robert Chambers's correspondents wrote to him when he was compiling his "Popular Rhymes of Scotland" as follows: "An old lady of my acquaintance used seriously to warn young women against being married in green, for she attributed her own misfortunes solely to having approached the altar of Hymen in a gown of that colour, which she had worn against the advice of her seniors, all of whom recommended blue as the lucky colour."

ENTERING THE WORLD FROM SUNDAY TO SATURDAY

It matters a good deal on what day of the week a child is born.

"Monday's child is fair of face,
  Tuesday's child is full of grace,
  Wednesday's child is full of woe,
  Thursday's child has far to go,
  Friday's child is loving and giving,
  Saturday's child must work hard for his living.
  The child of Sunday and Christmas Day
  Is good, and fair, and wise, and gay."

There is an old saying that if a man is born on a Sunday he will live without trouble all his life. "This is true enough," an intimate friend has remarked to us. "I was born on a Sunday, and up to the present moment, having gone through over half a century of existence, I cannot recollect having had five minutes of real trouble about anything."

INFANT VISITORS ✦

If you wish well to your neighbour's child, when it first comes to your house you must give it a cake, a little salt, and an egg.

CHILDREN SHOULD CRY WHEN BAPTIZED ✦

For children to cry when they are baptized is a good sign. It is an indication, for one thing, that they will be *good singers*.

TAKE THE BOYS TO THE FONT FIRST ✦

If several children are baptized together, if the girls are taken to the font before the boys, the boys will have no beards when they are men.

ROSEMARY DETERS THIEVES ✦

A sprig of rosemary in the house is good to keep off thieves. This shrub grows best in the garden where the lady rules the roast. "That be rosemary, sir," said a cottager in Hertfordshire; "they say it only grows where the missus is master, and it do grow here like wildfire."

SIGN THAT STRANGERS ARE COMING ✦

If you sneeze on a Saturday night after the lamp or gas is lighted you will during the incoming week see a stranger you never saw before.

❧ UNLUCKY OMENS ❧

BREAKING A LOOKING-GLASS

To break a looking-glass is a bad omen. Some say it causes seven years of sorrow; others that it is a sign that a member of the family will shortly die.

Most readers are no doubt acquainted with Bonaparte's belief in the bad fortune that goes with breaking a looking-glass. During one of his campaigns in Italy he broke the glass over Josephine's portrait. So disturbed was he at this ominous occurrence, and so strong was the impression made upon his mind that she might be dead, that he never rested until the return of the courier whom he had forthwith despatched to convince himself of her safety.

BEWARE OF SALT

To scatter salt by overturning the vessel in which it is contained is very unlucky. To some extent the evil may be averted by throwing a pinch of salt over the left shoulder.

Help no one to Salt. It is unlucky to help another person to salt. To whom the ill-luck is to happen does not seem to be settled, so it is as well for both to be careful. "Help me to salt, help me to sorrow," says the proverb.

LAYING ONE'S KNIFE CROSSWAYS

It is unlucky to lay one's knife and fork crossways; crosses and misfortunes being likely to follow therefrom.

PUTTING SHOES ON

The accidental putting on of the left shoe on the right foot or the right shoe on the left foot may be taken as the precursor of some unlucky accident.

To take off or put on the left shoe before the right is unlucky.

BREAKAGES

If you break anything fate will pursue you till you break two things more. The best way out of the difficulty is at once to break two matches.

GETTING OUT OF BED

Getting out of bed backwards makes things go wrong for the day.

WHEN MEAT IS BOILED

If meat shrinks in the pot when boiling it is unlucky; if it swells it is a sign of prosperity.

DON'T WALK UNDER A LADDER

To walk under a ladder is unlucky. According to some, it is a sign that you will be hanged, but this is to exaggerate the ill-luck.

STARTING ON A JOURNEY

When starting on a journey take care to put the right foot first; to make the first step with the left foot is not good luck.

AN UNLUCKY RETURN

You will meet with misfortune if you start to go out and have to return for something you forgot, unless you sit down for a minute or so before you go out again.

MEETING A SQUINTING WOMAN

To meet a squinting woman is unlucky unless you talk to her, which breaks the charm.

AN UNWELCOME MEETING ⚜

It is unlucky to meet a funeral procession; but the omen may be counteracted by taking off your hat, which is intended as a mark of respect to the evil spirits who may be hovering about the corpse.

WHISTLING WOMEN ⚜

It is unlucky for women to whistle. This has been the way ever since, when the nails of our Lord's cross were being forged, a woman stood by and whistled.

BEFORE EATING AN EGG ⚜

To break the small end of an egg is unlucky.

SWEEPING AT NIGHT ⚜

A good housewife will never sweep the floor at night. Should circumstances ever compel her to do so she will sweep the dirt into a corner, and not lift it till the morning. Any other course will lead to misfortune.

STUMBLING IS UNLUCKY ❈

Stumbling at a grave is a bad sign.

Stumbling when going upstairs is a lucky sign, but to stumble when going down is one of the worst signs possible.

SWEEPING LUCK OUTDOORS ❈

Never sweep the rooms of a house immediately after one of the inmates has set out on a journey; this will sweep out all the luck with him.

SNEEZING ❈

Sneezing to the left is unlucky, but prosperous to the right.

When any one sneezes it is the right thing, in case of ill-luck, to say "God bless you!"

NOSE BLEEDING ❈

A single drop of blood from the nose commonly foretells either death or a very severe fit of illness; three drops being still more ominous.

SHAKING HANDS

It is unlucky to shake hands across a table.

When two people are shaking hands, if two others of the company attempt to shake hands across their hands it is a very unlucky sign, and indicates a rupture of friendship.

GOING IN BY THE BACK-DOOR

It is unlucky to enter a house which you are going to occupy by the back-door.

GIVING SHARP OR CUTTING INSTRUMENTS

It is unlucky to give a knife, scissors, razor, or any sharp or cutting instrument to one's mistress or friend, as they are apt to cut love or friendship. The ill effects of such a present, however, may be counteracted by our taking some trifle in return – a farthing, a pebble, an oyster-shell, or such like.

CHILDREN! DO NOT WALK BACKWARDS

Children ought to be cautioned by their parents not to walk backwards when going an errand; it is a sure sign that they will be unfortunate in their objects.

SINGING BEFORE BREAKFAST

If you sing before breakfast you will cry before supper.

YOU WILL WEEP SOON

Should your eyelid quiver, that is an unlucky omen: you will weep before long.

THE LOOKING-GLASS

It is unlucky to see one's face in a glass by candle-light.

LOSING THE WEDDING-RING

If a wife loses her wedding-ring it is a sign that she will sooner or later lose her husband's affection.

LETTER WRITING

The mistake of a word in a letter is a sure omen that whatever request it contains will be refused.

LUCKY OMENS

RISING ON THE RIGHT SIDE
To rise on the right side is accounted lucky.

FINDING MONEY
To find a piece of money is a very fortunate circumstance.

FINDING A HORSESHOE
It is very lucky to find a horse-shoe, and all the more lucky if the shoe is studded with nails.

WHAT THE TEETH TELL
To have teeth far apart is a sign that one will be fortunate and see a great deal of the world.

BORN TO BE RICH
Persons with much hair or down upon their arms and hands will at some future period enjoy great wealth; or, as the common expression has it, "they are born to be rich."

A LUCKY COIN
The luckiest coin to give away is a bent one. A copper coin with a hole made through it is also a lucky coin.

THROWING THE SHOE

To throw an old shoe after any person when we wish him to succeed in what he is going about is lucky. For this reason an old shoe is often thrown after the bride and bridegroom on their leaving the church or the *maison paternelle* after the wedding.

MONEY AND GIFTS ARE ON THE WAY

The itching of the right-hand palm portends the reception of a gift; which is rendered more certain if this advice be followed –

> "Rub it 'gainst wood,
> Tis sure to come good."

If, however, the left palm itches, it is a less cheerful sign, and betokens that you are about to pay money.

THE SLEEPING CHILD

A knife placed near a sleeping child is a lucky omen.

SOMETHING IMPORTANT ABOUT DAYS

ONE day is not as good as another. They vary in excellence, and an undertaking which would turn out prosperous if started upon, say, the 10th of May, might have a very unfortunate ending if begun upon, say, the 15th of August.

THE DAYS OF THE WEEK

- Tuesday and Wednesday are lucky days.
- Thursday has one lucky hour, viz., the hour before the sun rises.
- Friday is unlucky. Monday and Saturday and Sunday are neutral days, of which in regard to luck it is often, indeed, almost always, difficult to affirm either one thing or another.

UNLUCKY FRIDAY

Friday is in all countries, to say the least of it, a peculiar day. In this country it is unlucky, and upon it no undertaking of importance should be commenced. It is not a propitious day for setting out on a voyage or a journey, or entering on a new situation, or indeed for making a start with anything whatever, matrimony in Scotland alone excepted. Neither is it a good day for "going a-courting."

It is remarkable that there is a difference between England and Scotland in regard to matrimonial ventures begun on a Friday. There is some mysterious cause for it no doubt in England.

Friday is certainly not a lucky day south of the Border on which to start matrimonial life; but in Scotland Friday is the lucky day of the week for marriages. It is a well-established fact that a large proportion of the marriages in Glasgow, for example, are celebrated on Friday.

DAYS FOR NEW CLOTHES

If a person have his measure taken for new clothes on a Sunday it is very bad luck. If on a Monday he will be fortunate. If on a Tuesday he may expect accidents by fire. If on a Wednesday he will enjoy happiness and tranquillity. If on a Thursday he will be called to travel both by land and sea. If on a Friday a death will happen amongst his nearest relations. If on a Saturday he will shortly receive a handsome legacy.

DO NOT CUT YOUR NAILS ON A SUNDAY

It makes a considerable difference whether a man cuts his nails on a Sunday or puts it off till another day.

"Cut them on Monday, cut them for health;
Cut them on Tuesday, cut them for wealth;
Cut them on Wednesday, cut for a letter;
Cut them on Thursday, for something better;
Cut them on Friday, you cut for a wife;
Cut them on Saturday, cut for long life;
Cut them on Sunday, you cut them for evil,
For all that week you'll be ruled by the devil."

Another version gives the last two lines —
"A man had better ne'er be born,
Than have his nails on a Sunday shorn."

BEST TO SNEEZE ON SATURDAY

"If you sneeze on Monday, you sneeze for danger;
Sneeze on a Tuesday, kiss a stranger;
Sneeze on a Wednesday, sneeze for a letter;
Sneeze on a Thursday, something better;
Sneeze on a Friday, sneeze for sorrow;
Sneeze on a Saturday, see your sweetheart to-morrow."

OMENS FOR LOVERS

DAYS FOR LOVERS
There are many opportunities during the course of the twelve months for obtaining the guidance of the powers of mystery in connection with one's love affairs.

NEW YEAR'S DAY (JANUARY 1ST). His or Her Christian Name? – The Christian name of the first person one sees of the opposite sex on New Year's Day will be the name of one's future husband or wife.

ON THE EVE OF ST. AGNES (JANUARY 20TH). St. Agnes, the patron of purity, whose day is the 21st of January, has from time immemorial been invoked by love-sick damsels, anxious to obtain some knowledge of their future husbands.

ON ST. VALENTINE'S DAY (FEBRUARY 14TH). Learning One's Destiny – The first unmarried person of the other sex whom you see on the morning of St. Valentine's Day is your destined wife or your destined husband.

ALL HALLOWS' EVE, OR HALLOWEEN (OCTOBER 31ST). The leading idea of this famous festival is that it is the time of all others when supernatural influences prevail. Divination then attains its highest power, and then, if ever, we can obtain authentic information in regard to our love affairs.

MARRIED LIFE BEGUN AS IT SHOULD BE

N an affair of such importance as taking the first steps in wedded happiness – or the reverse – it is as well that the wisdom of our ancestors is at our disposal. Wise readers still unmarried will treasure up for future reference what is here set down, and may one of these days look back on their first acquaintance with the following notes as one of the fortunate circumstances of their lives.

WHEN TO MARRY

To marry in Lent is very unlucky –

> "If you marry in Lent
> You will live to repent."

MAY IS AN UNLUCKY MONTH FOR MARRIAGES. A bachelor, on this, remarks that the other unlucky months are June, July, August, September, October, November, December, January, February, March, and April.

JUNE AND OCTOBER are the most propitious months of all the twelve for marriage, and a happy result is rendered doubly certain if the ceremony is timed to take place at the full moon or when the sun and moon are in conjunction.

IF ONE DAY OF THE YEAR IS TO BE SELECTED for marriage before another let it be the 4th day of June. Next to that stands the 9th of October, a day of the brightest promise in the calendar of Cupid.

THE DAYS OF THE WEEK VARY IN EXCELLENCE for taking this important step. Their values will be easily remembered by any one who will take the trouble to learn the following rhyme –

"Monday for wealth,
Tuesday for health,
Wednesday the best day of all;
Thursday for crosses,
Friday for losses,
Saturday no luck at all."

BEWARE OF THE LOOKING-GLASS

It is unlucky for a bride on her wedding-day to look in the glass when she is completely dressed before starting for church. Care should be taken to put on a glove or some slight article of adornment after the last look has been taken in the mirror.

HAPPY OMENS

The sneezing of a cat is a lucky omen to a bride who is to be married the following day. Her casting eyes on a strange cat is also a very good sign.

The bride who dreams of fairies the night before her marriage will be thrice blessed.

LUCK IN THE WEDDING DRESS

To be lucky the bride must wear –

"Something old and something new,
  Something gold and something blue."

Should a girl find a spider on her wedding dress she may consider herself uncommonly fortunate. No girl who would be a happy bride must take a hand in the making of her wedding cake or the sewing of her bridal gown.

AN UNHAPPY OMEN

It is an unhappy omen for a wedding to be put off when the day has been fixed.

ON THE WAY TO CHURCH

The best and most fortunate homes are always those which start with a wedding on a bright sunshiny day. "Happy is the bride," says the proverb, "that the sun shines on."

No bride or groom should be given a telegram while on the way to church. It is a sign of evil.

THE WEDDING RING

Whatever ring a bride is married with she should take care it is not a diamond ring. That is to be avoided, says an old writer, "because the diamond hinders the roundness of the ring, ending the infiniteness thereof, and seems to presage some termination in their love, which ought ever to endure."

To try on a wedding ring before the ceremony is unpropitious. Should the shaking hand of the groom drop this symbol of love in the act of putting it on the bride's finger, *the ceremony had better be stopped right there.* To lose it is prophetic of evil, and to remove it after it is placed on the finger is unlucky.

THE FINGER FOR THE WEDDING RING

The wedding ring is almost invariably placed on the fourth finger of the left hand, and all because many centuries ago the Egyptians believed that a certain small artery proceeded directly from the heart to the termination of that digit.

IN LEAVING THE CHURCH

In leaving the church the bride should be very careful to put her right foot foremost, and on no account allow any one to speak to her husband until she has called him by name.

Be sure when you get married that you don't go in at one door and out at another, or you will always be unlucky.

TEARS OF GOOD FORTUNE

It is not a good sign if a bride *fails to shed tears* on her wedding-day.

HINTS TO THE BRIDEGROOM

On the wedding day if the bride drops her handkerchief and the bridegroom politely picks it up, it is an omen that he will play second fiddle during his married life.

If the bridegroom carries a miniature horseshoe in his pocket he will always in his married life have good luck.

THROWING THE SHOE

Both when leaving the church and when starting for her wedding tour, an old shoe or slipper should be thrown after the bride for luck.

WHEAT AND RICE

Sprinkling the bride with wheat brings good luck. So also does sprinkling her with rice.

A NOTE FOR THE BRIDESMAIDS

When the bridesmaids undress the bride they must throw away and lose all the pins. Woe to the bride if a single one is left about her. Nothing will go right. Woe also to the bridesmaids if they keep one of them, for they will not be married before Whitsuntide or until the Easter following at the soonest.

ENTERING HER NEW HOME

When the bride enters her new home it is a good and lucky practice to *break a cake over her head*. Care should be taken that it is not done over the head of any other person, which would be a singularly bad omen.

WILL BRIDE OR BRIDEGROOM DIE FIRST?

The first to kneel down at the altar – be it bridegroom or bride – is sure to die first.

MARRIAGES ON BOARD SHIP

Ship marriages are considered anything but lucky. Get married on land or don't get married at all.

IN THE COUNTRY

TAKE COURAGE!
Magical arts cannot be practised so well upon persons in the open air as in houses.

DO NOT GO TO SLEEP IN A BEAN-FIELD
This is a very unlucky proceeding. Those who go to sleep in a bean-field, especially if their slumbers are prolonged beyond sundown, have awful dreams and often go crazy.

WHIPS AND STICKS MAY DO HARM
It is not good to crack a whip or swing about a stick aimlessly. Do not do it, for who knows what is in the air?

AT THE VILLAGE STILE
At certain places the devil exerts a stronger influence than at others, and this is most perceptible in narrow and difficult ways. A village stile is a favourite resort of the adversary, and when, under such circumstances, an unfortunate wight attempts the surmounting, he may find his efforts fruitless, till he has turned some article of clothing inside out.

THE WITCH IN THE DAIRY

There is no place about a farmhouse in which witches work more mischief than in the dairy. Their baneful powers are there exercised to the discomfort and annoyance of all industrious dairymaids.

To keep them out the best protection undoubtedly is the horseshoe over the door or a sprig of the mountain ash or rowan-tree hung up in full view of all possible visitors. In other sections we have spoken of the virtues of both horseshoes and sprigs of mountain-ash. Should the witch, however, gain entrance, to expel her from the churn put a red-hot iron into the cream, or throw salt into the fire before you begin to churn. The butter then will come, and everything be just as it ought to be.

AT SEA

IMPORTANT NOTES FOR FISHERMEN
When putting out to sea for fishing it is not lucky to communicate one's intention to one's neighbour. When fishermen are on the way to their boats, *should they meet a pig* they should turn back. A pig under such circumstances is an unlucky sign, indicating possibly a storm and at the very least a poor catch.

SURE TO BE DROWNED
The old clothes of a fisherman should never be mended with needle and thread on Sunday; if this is done the owner is sure to be drowned.

WANTED, A GOOD BREEZE ✦

In a dead calm whistling is the best of all methods by which to induce the wind to come. To whistle at sea, however, when there is no necessity for it is highly objectionable; the breeze then blowing may become much stronger than is either agreeable or safe.

BEWARE WHAT YOU DO ✦

When on the ocean one should beware of seals. Witches have often been known to change themselves into seals and follow mariners and fishermen. To throw a cat overboard or drown one at sea is very unlucky; it is a sure way indeed to raise a deadly storm.

ON DEATH

EATH is sure, but as the when and the manner of it are uncertain, the following notes will prove useful to all who desire to know something regarding their own passage and that of their friends through the dark portal which leads to another existence.

WHEN YOU MAY EXPECT SOMEONE TO DIE

THE WHINING OF A FAVOURITE DOG is a sign of approaching calamity to the family to which it belongs.

IF THE CLOCK STRIKES while the text is being given out in church on a Sunday, a death may be expected in the parish.

WHEN ANY ONE IS ILL and a sudden knock is heard for which there is apparently no possible cause, then we may expect the speedy end of life to the sufferer.

TO HAVE A LONG SUCCESSION OF BLACK CARDS dealt to a person while at play is prophetic of death to himself or some member of the family.

WILL LIFE BE LONG OR SHORT?

To find out whether any one will live long throw a lock of his or her hair on the fire. If it burns brightly it is a sure sign that he or she will reach a good old age. The brighter the flame the longer the life.

THE BANSHEE GIVES WARNING

In the last century every great family in Ireland had a banshee who attended regularly, but of late years their visits have been few and far between. The banshee is a sort of aristocratic fairy, who, in the shape of a little, hideous old woman, has been known to appear and sing, in a mournful, supernatural voice, under the windows of great houses, to warn the family that some of them are soon to die.

A PROCESSION OF THOSE ABOUT TO DIE

If a person have the hardihood to place himself within the porch of the church, or in a position which commands the church door, on the ghostly eve of St. Mark – St. Mark's Day being the 25th of April – he will see the souls of those whose bodies are to be buried at that church the following year approach the building in the dead waste and middle of the night. The doors are flung open by some invisible hand just at twelve o'clock, and the spirits enter in the rotation their mortal bodies are to die in.

DYING FAR FROM HOME

The spirits of people about to die, especially if they are in distant parts of the earth, often return to their friends, and thus predict the calamity. While the spirit is thus away the person dying is supposed by those around him to be in a swoon.

NO DYING ON PIGEONS' OR GAME FEATHERS

No person can die when lying either on pigeons' feathers or on game feathers.

IN THE CHURCHYARD

TAKE AN ELDER BUSH AND TRIM IT into the form of a cross, then plant it on a newly-made grave; should it bloom after that it is a sign that the soul of the dead person is happy.

A SHIVERING SENSATION suddenly felt in your back is a sign that some one is walking over your future grave.

IT IS BAD LUCK to walk by accident over the graves of the dead.

THE MURDERER DETECTED

The corpse or bones of a murdered person will bleed on being touched by whoever was guilty of the murder.

CHAPTER TWO

WHAT WE MAY LEARN FROM ANIMALS

❧ DOMESTIC ANIMALS ❧

MAY CATS
Cats born in the month of May are good for catching neither mice nor rats. They are unlucky too to have about the house, and will *suck the breath of children*.

THE BEST MOUSERS
These are cats that have been stolen.

PUSS WITH HER BACK TO THE FIRE
To allow the cat to sit with her back to the fire is unlucky.

A LUCKY OMEN
A kitten coming to a house is a lucky omen.

THE LATTER END OF CATS
Any one wilfully or accidentally killing a cat will be punished by seven years of unhappiness.

CATS IN WITCHCRAFT
- Black cats, in case they should be witches, should never be allowed to go near the cradles of young children.
- Witches in the shape of cats are in the habit of roaming about the roofs of houses, especially during the month of February.
- When a cat looks weak and thin it may arise from its being ridden on by witches at night.
- Cats should be carefully shut up on All Hallows' Eve, the

31ˢᵗ of October. Those cats that contrive to escape incarceration that night "may be seen, by those brave enough to look out, scampering over hill and dale and across the lonely moors, each one ridden by a brownie, a bogie, a spunkie, or some other infernal jockey."

RATS

To see a white rat is a token of good fortune.

If rats gnaw a man's clothes it is a great sign of ill-luck.

Rats have a presentiment of coming evil, and always take care to desert in time a ship about to be wrecked, or a house about to be flooded or burned.

MICE

A number of mice suddenly coming into a house is an omen of death. For a mouse to run over any person and to squeak behind the bed of an invalid also foretells death.

When starting on a journey it is unlucky to meet with a shrew.

A STRANGE DOG

A strange dog following you is a sign of good luck.

A HOWLING DOG

The howling of a dog at night indicates approaching death to those who may be ill in the neighbourhood.

WORKING BEASTS

LUCKY HORSES

If a horse has a white star on its forehead that is a lucky sign.

To meet a piebald horse is lucky, and if you meet two in succession you have but to express any reasonable wish and it will be gratified within a few days.

AN UNLUCKY HORSE

It is a sign of "bad luck" to meet a white horse, *unless the person spits at it*; which action averts the ill consequences.

HORSES SEE SPIRITS

Horses are able to see spirits. The exhibition by them of signs of terror when no cause of alarm is noticeable by human vision is an omen of death.

WHEN A HORSE NEIGHS

In warfare the neighing of a horse is a sure pledge of coming victory, and his silence is an indication of defeat. At the battle of Agincourt, in 1415, the French augured badly for their success from the fact that their horses had not neighed the night before.

COWS

An ox or a cow breaking into a garden is an omen of death.

Should a farmer's cows become restive without any apparent cause it forebodes trouble to either the master or the mistress.

LAMBS AND COLTS

For the first lamb or colt you see in the season to have its tail towards you is unlucky.

PIGS

If a pig is killed in the wane of the moon the bacon is sure to shrink in the boiling; if, on the other hand, the pig is killed when the moon is at the full, the bacon will swell.

HARES

To have a hare cross the road in front of any one who is going on an errand is not lucky. Under such a circumstance it is wisest to turn back and not pursue one's business till the next meal has been eaten, for beyond that the evil influence does not extend.

✦ LITTLE CREATURES ✦

AN UNLUCKY SIGN ✦
To see three butterflies together is unlucky.

"LET THE SPIDER RUN ALIVE." ✦
It is not lucky to injure a spider.

> "If you wish to live and thrive,
>   Let the spider run alive."

The favour with which the spider is regarded perhaps arises from the influence of an old legend which tells how, when our Saviour lay in the manger at Bethlehem, a spider came and span a web over Him as a protection against surrounding dangers.

The bustling housekeeper should take note that if she kills a spider she may calculate on breaking a piece of crockery or glass before the day comes to an end.

If the little red spider known as the "money spider" is found on any one's clothes, it is a sign that he or she will shortly have money.

WHAT COMES OF KILLING A WASP

The first wasp seen in the season, like the first butterfly, as we have just mentioned, should always be killed. By so doing you secure to yourself good luck and freedom from enemies throughout the year.

ABOUT BUTTERFLIES

Not to catch and kill the first butterfly seen in spring is unlucky – and the ill-luck will last until spring comes round again.

CRICKETS BRING GOOD FORTUNE

The cheerful cricket is always lucky in a house, and should be most carefully preserved. Their presence is a sure omen of prosperity, and to kill one, even accidentally, is one of the worst things that could happen.

MAKING A SNAIL OF USE

If black snails are seized by the horns and tossed over the left shoulder, the process will insure good luck to the person who does so.

PREDICTIONS OF THE DEATH WATCH

The clicking of the insect known as the death-watch is an omen of the decease of some one in the house in which it is heard.

BEES KNOW MORE THAN PEOPLE THINK

ALL who have watched bees are aware that they are knowing little creatures, with whims and caprices, and a close connection with the fortunes of the human race.

BEES DETEST QUARRELSOME PEOPLE

They are lovers of peace, and will not thrive with a quarrelsome family. If the wife nags at the husband or the husband bullies the wife, it is a wonder if the bees do not leave them – they often do.

Especially is it offensive to the bees if they themselves are the subject of quarrel.

BUYING AND STEALING

When bees are purchased the swarm should be paid for in gold; silver coin is unlucky for the purpose. For this reason the buyer should take care to have at least half a sovereign handy in his pocket. Stolen hives will never thrive, but pine away and die.

CHRISTMAS FARE FOR BEES

It promotes good feeling to put a little sugar at the hive's entrance on Christmas Eve. At the stroke of midnight the bees will be found coming out to eat it.

BEES MUST BE TOLD OF A DEATH IN THE FAMILY

When there is a death in the family where bees are kept, the bees should be informed of the event, otherwise they will leave their hives and never return. Some people put wine and honey at the same time before the hives, but this is understood not to be absolutely necessary. The rule is to tap quietly three times on all the hives in succession and say, "Little brownie, little brownie, your master (or naming the person) is dead." Then the bees begin to hum by way of showing their consent to remain.

On the day of the funeral the bees should be put in mourning by placing a scarf of black crape on each hive.

AN UNLUCKY SIGN

Should a swarm of bees settle on one's premises without the owner coming to lay claim to them, it is unlucky. It is also a bad sign if a swarm of bees alight on a dead tree, or the dead branch of a living tree; it indicates, in fact, that there will probably be a death in the family of the owner during the year.

ANOTHER UNLUCKY SIGN

The entrance of a wild or bumble bee into a house is a certain sign of death.

FEATHERED PROPHETS
OF GOOD AND EVIL

UNLUCKY TO HARM ROBINS AND WRENS

The robin is a sacred bird: to kill one is little less than sacrilege, and its eggs are free from the destroying hand of the bird-nester. It is asserted that the respect shown to it by man is joined in by the animals of the wood. The weasel and wild-cat, it is said, will neither molest it nor eat it when killed.

The wren is not perhaps so much spoken about as the robin, but it is nevertheless a bird whose favour it is desirable to secure.

"The robin and the wren
Be God A'mighty's cock and hen."

Whilst ill-treatment is sure to be avenged, kindness shown to these birds is as certainly repaid.

The reason why the robin redbreast is the favourite of man is that while our Saviour was bearing His cross, one of these birds, they say, took a thorn from His crown, which dyed its breast; and ever since that time robin redbreasts have been the friends of the human race.

A SINGING CANARY

When a canary sings cheerfully it is a good sign, but when it becomes silent and remains so there is a great probability of approaching misfortune.

SWALLOWS AND MARTINS

Swallows or martins building in a window corner, or indeed anywhere about a house, is a lucky omen, and any trouble they cause should be patiently borne, seeing that their presence causes prosperity. The more birds the luckier.

To tear down a nest is a daring of the fates sure to be followed by a calamity within a twelvemonth.

Swallows and martins are never found coming to a house where there is strife.

BAD SIGNS

When swallows and martins forsake a house they have once frequented the occupier must expect misfortune.

NOT ALWAYS TO BE RELIED ON

An eagle hovering over one is as a general rule a sign of approaching success in some important enterprise, but it is not a sign invariably to be relied on.

PIGEONS AS A SIGN OF DEATH

If a pigeon is seen sitting in a tree, or comes into the house, or from being wild suddenly becomes tame, it is a sign of death.

If an invalid asks for pigeons to eat it is a sign of approaching death.

WHEN SPRINKLED WITH PIGEON'S BLOOD

He who is sprinkled with pigeon's blood will never die a natural death. A sculptor, in the days of Charles I, was carrying home a bust of that monarch. Just at that moment a pigeon overhead was struck by a hawk, and the blood of the bird fell on the neck of the bust. The sculptor thought it ominous, and sure enough Charles I came to be beheaded.

UNLUCKY FEATHERS

Peacocks' feathers in a house are unlucky. They form the emblem of an evil eye or an ever-watchful traitor.

AN OMINOUS BIRD

The owl is the most ominous of all birds, and its screech is to be heard with alarm.

≈ Crows and Magpies ≈

CROWS IN DAYS OF YORE

The crow is called by Pliny a bird of ill-omened garrulity, most inauspicious at the time of incubation, or just after the summer solstice. The appearance of a flight of crows upon the left of their camp sufficed to cow the courage of the soldiers of old Rome, since they looked upon it as a sure sign of defeat – as sure as when the birds hovered or passed over their standard.

DEATH IS SURE ❦

A crow croaking thrice as he flies over a house is a sure prognostic of the death of some member of the family.

COUNT THEIR NUMBER ❦

Whether a lucky or an unlucky inference is to be drawn from seeing crows depends on their number.

"One's unlucky, two's lucky,
Three is health, four is wealth,
Five is sickness, and six is death."

AN EVIL OMEN ❦

A single magpie crossing your path is an evil omen. But the evil influence may be averted by laying two straws across, or by describing the figure of a cross on the ground.

ONE, TWO, THREE, AND FOUR ❦

Like the crow, the magpie is not always an ill-omened bird. It altogether depends on the number you see.

"One for sorrow, two for mirth,
Three for a wedding, four for death."

In the Poultry Yard

CROWING HENS ARE UNLUCKY

The crowing of a hen bodes evil, and is frequently followed by the death of some member of the family. No house can thrive whose hens are addicted to this kind of amusement. Hence the old proverb often quoted –

> "A whistling woman and a crowing hen
> Are neither fit for God nor men."

A COCK MAY CROW TO ANNOUNCE A STRANGER

When a cock crows with his head in at the door, or even turned towards the door, that is the attitude of a prophetic bird: it is as much as to say, "You may look for the arrival of a stranger."

THE POULTRY KNOW THAT DEATH IS NEAR

Before the death of a farmer his poultry frequently go to roost at noon-day instead of at the usual time.

THE EGGS IN THE NEST ✦

In what is technically termed "setting a hen," care should be taken that the nest is composed of an odd number of eggs, or else the chickens will not prosper. Each egg should be marked with a little black cross: this is instrumental in producing good chickens, and it acts as a charm to prevent attacks from weasels or other farmyard marauders.

WHEN DEALING WITH EGGS ✦

It is unlucky to bring eggs into the house after sunset.

Should eggs be brought over running water there is no use attempting to hatch them, for they contain no chickens.

It is unlucky to sell eggs after sunset.

DO NOT BURN EGG-SHELLS: CRUSH THEM UP ✦

Never burn egg-shells; if you do, the hens cease to lay.

Empty egg-shells should always be crushed up. The reason for this is to prevent witchcraft. If the shells are left whole there is a chance that *witches will use them as boats, and so put to sea and wreck ships.*

❧ The Cuckoo ❧

THE CUCKOO "TELLS NO LIES."
Whatever you may be doing when first you hear the cry
"Cuckoo," that you will be chiefly doing all through the year.
Above all, if you do not wish to pass the year idle, run round
in a circle as soon as you have heard its notes.

It is on the whole luckiest to hear the cuckoo for the first
time in spring when you are walking. As the Scottish saying
has it, "Gang and hear the gowk (cuckoo) yell, and it will be
a happy year with you."

WEALTH AND WISHES
When the cry of the cuckoo is heard for the first time in spring,
it is customary to turn the money in the pocket. Doing so is a
protection against being hard up during all the year. If you
have only a penny in your pocket, turn it over, and you will
never be without one until you hear him again. In reference to
this pecuniary idea respecting the cuckoo, the children sing –
"Cuckoo, cuckoo, cherry-tree,
  Catch a penny and give it to me."
Besides turning your money you ought also to wish, and if
your wish is within the bounds of reason it is sure to be fulfilled.

HOW LONG WE HAVE TO LIVE
The most singular feature in the cuckoo is its power of telling
people how long they have to live. If when you first hear the
cuckoo of a morning you put the question in a respectful
manner, it will repeat its note just as many times as you have
years yet to spend in this world.

CHAPTER THREE

USEFUL CHARMS AND SPELLS

MAGICAL REMEDIES

A GENERAL REMEDY

To fan the face of a patient with leaves taken from the Bible will go a long way towards the cure of most cases of illness.

ADDER'S BITE: A CERTAIN CURE

A certain remedy for the bite of an adder is to kill the offending reptile, and apply some of its fat to the wound.

ANAEMIA

For this condition, in which there is an impoverished state of the blood, the patient being very pale, there is a simple remedy. To have ruddy cheeks, *bury a drop of your blood under a rose-bush.*

BLEEDING AT THE NOSE

If a man suffers from bleeding at the nose, he asks a woman to buy him a lace (if a woman, she asks a man), without either giving money, saying what it is wanted for, or returning thanks when it is received. The lace so obtained must be worn round the neck for the space of nine days, at the expiration of which the patient will experience no return of the disorder.

HEADACHE ❧

If you *wear a snake's skin round your head* you will never have the headache.

NETTLE-STINGS ❧

When one is stung by a nettle, take a dock-leaf, and with it rub the part affected, all the while repeating –

> "Nettle in, dock out;
> Dock in, nettle out;
> Nettle in, dock out;
> Dock rub nettle out."

RHEUMATISM ❧

A *potato begged or stolen* is a preservative against rheumatism. Sufferers from this complaint should observe that the small knuckle-bone of a ham carried in the pocket is a charm against the evil eye in general and rheumatism in particular.

TEETHING ❧

Mothers whose children are troubled with teething should read this –

> "The vicar of a village in East Sussex was rather surprised the other day by one of his most respectable parishioners telling him that she never had any trouble with her children teething. Directly they showed any signs of it she borrowed a neighbour's donkey, set the child backwards on the cross of the donkey's neck, and led it while she repeated the Lord's Prayer, and she never had any more trouble. 'Do I, Jim?' she wound up, appealing to her husband, who stolidly agreed."

WARTS

Rub the warts with a cinder. The cinder tied up in paper and dropped where four roads meet will transfer the warts to whoever opens the packet. Alternatively, *steal a piece of meat, rub your warts with it, then hide the meat,* and as it decays, so will your warts; or rub them with a bean-pod, then throw the pod away, and as it decays, so will your warts.

WHOOPING-COUGH

Whooping-cough will never be taken by any child which has ridden upon a bear. While bear-baiting was in fashion, great part of the owner's profits arose from the money given by parents whose children had a ride.

WOUNDS

The ring-finger – the fourth finger of the left hand – is the favoured finger for curative purposes; it has the power of curing any sore or wound which is stroked by it.

TALISMANS & AMULETS

TALISMANS

Talismans generally consist, or at any rate ought to consist, of an astrological character engraved upon a sympathetic stone or on the metal corresponding to the constellation or the star represented; they are fashioned at the auspicious hour marked by the ascending of the star or planet whose influence is conjoined with them, and they act by the power of the astral spirit to whom they are thus dedicated.

The chief virtue of the talisman is in averting disease and the influence of evil spirits.

AMULETS

Amulets have nearly the same virtues as talismans, but they are of less potent effect, as they must always be worn on the person to do any service.

Any material will do for an amulet, but for the more universal amulets *precious stones* are naturally preferred, as they serve for elegance in dress, and there are few diseases capable of resisting their virtues, provided only they are formed in the propitious hour of their planets' ascendency.

Verses from the Bible, and especially from the Gospel of St. John, are of great power as amulets.

AGAINST THE EVIL EYE

THE EYE OF ENVY ⋟

The evil eye obtains its power from the envious disposition that lies behind it. It emits a malignant and poisonous spirit, which has a disastrous effect on the person on whom the eye is cast. The more wicked any person is the more power has he to exercise the evil eye.

CHILDREN CHIEFLY SUFFER ⋟

Those chiefly in danger from the influence of the evil eye are children, but it may be exercised on all persons and things.

Children in unwashed baby linen are easily subject to the influence of the evil eye; so also, says an old writer, "is any fair one who employs two lady's maids to dress her hair." To these must be added "all who lie in bed very late in the morning, especially if they wear night-caps; and all who break their fast on cheese or peas."

SYMPTOMS OF ITS INFLUENCE

The signs of any one being under the influence of the evil eye are loss of colour, heavy and melancholy eyes, either overflowing with tears or unnaturally dry, frequent sighs and lowness of spirits, watchfulness, bad dreams, falling away of flesh.

A SURE TEST

In order to ascertain whether a child is fascinated – under the spell, that is to say, of the evil eye – three oak apples may be *dropped into a basin of water under its cradle*, the person who drops them observing the strictest silence. If they swim the child is free; if they sink it is affected.

CHARMS AGAINST THE EVIL EYE

There are many charms which protect against the evil eye. Amongst the best are *sweeping a child's face with the bough of a pine-tree; laying a piece of turf cut from a boy's grave under a boy's pillow*; from a girl's under a girl's; hanging up the key of the house over a child's cradle; or *hanging round its neck* fennel seeds or *bread and cheese*.

A YOUTH IN DANGER

If a youth sits musing and intently looking into the fire it is often a sign that some one has cast the evil eye on him, or is fascinating him for evil. In case this should be so let any one without speaking take the tongs and turn the centre coal or piece of wood in the grate, and whilst doing so say, "God preserve us from all harm!" This will break the spell and cause the intended evil to revert to the ill-disposed person who was attempting mischief.

THE EVIL EYE CAST UPON CATTLE ✄

The evil eye has a singularly bad effect upon cattle, mischances frequently, and sometimes even deaths, being occasioned by its means.

A good charm for the protection of cattle is a small piece of mountain ash bound into a cow's tail. It is a wise plan to put boughs of mountain ash about the cow-houses, and if some honeysuckle is added it makes the protection even more certain.

SPELLS FOR LOVERS

To Know One's Future
~ Partner in Life ~

THE EVEN ASH LEAF CHARM
The following four lines are to be repeated by girls anxious to know their future. They must gather an even ash leaf, and holding it in the hand walk along the road saying –

"This even ash I carry in hand
The first I meet shall be my husband!
If he be single let him draw nigh,
But if he be married then he may pass by."

To ensure success the leaf is sometimes *thrown at* the passer-by.

YOU MAY MAKE USE OF A PIECE OF CLOVER
Another charm to be used by young men and maidens who wish to know who their future wives or husbands are to be is the following. The "Clover of two" means a piece of clover with only two leaves upon it.

"A Clover, a Clover of two,
Put it in your right shoe;
The first young man [woman] you meet,
In field, street or lane,
You'll have him [her] or one of his [her] name."

THE NEW MOON KNOWS IT

On the first appearance of the new moon let a girl go out and pluck a handful of grass, repeating –

"New moon, new moon, tell me if you can,
If I have here a hair like the hair of my guidman."

On returning indoors let the grass be carefully examined; if a hair is found amongst it, which is often the case, the colour of that hair indicates that of the future husband's.

THE SNAIL KNOWS IT

If a girl will take a snail and place it on a slate it will describe by its turning the initials of her future husband's name.

THE COLOUR OF HIS HAIR

When a country girl first sees the new moon in the new year she should take her stocking off one foot and run to the nearest stile. When she gets there she will find a hair between the great toe and the next, and it will be the colour of her lover's.

BY THE AID OF THE MOON

When a country girl first sees the new moon after Midsummer (June 24th) she should go to a stile, turn her back to it, and say –

"All hail, new moon, all hail to thee!
I prithee, good moon, reveal to me
This night who shall my true love be;
Who he is and what he wears,
And what he does all months and years."

She will then see the apparition of her lover.

BY APPLESEEDS

On the eve of St. Thomas's Day (the 20th of December) cut an apple in two and count the seeds in each half. If the number is even you will be married soon. If a seed be cut in two the course of true love will not run smoothly. If two be so cut it is a sign of approaching widowhood.

SEEN IN THE LOOKING-GLASS

If a girl wants to discover what sort of a husband will eventually lead her to the altar let her sit late on the eve of Christmas (the 24th of December) between two large mirrors. She must place a candle on either side and then watch till she can see twelve reflected candles. If the fates are propitious she ought also to discern the husband she desires portrayed in the glass before her.

VISITED IN DREAMS

A SIMPLE SPELL

If a girl would dream of her sweetheart let her write his name, as well as her own, on a piece of paper at twelve o'clock at night. Let her burn the paper, but carefully gather up the ashes, and lay them, closely wrapped in paper, on a piece of looking-glass, marked with the sign of the cross. This must be put under her pillow, when she is sure to dream of the object of her affections.

YARROW WILL CAUSE HIM TO COME

Pluck yarrow *from a young man's grave*, saying as you do so –

"Yarrow, sweet yarrow, the first that I have found,
And in the name of Jesus I pluck it from the ground,
As Joseph loved sweet Mary, and took her for his dear,
So in a dream this night, I hope my true love will appear."

Sleep with the yarrow under the pillow.

DREAM ON WEDDING-CAKE

To eat a piece of wedding-cake is a sure way of enabling one to see in a dream his or her future partner for life.

ON THE EVE OF ST. AGNES (JANUARY 20TH)

A girl should take her right leg stocking and knit her left garter round it, saying –

"I knit this knot, this knot I knit,
To know the thing I know not yet,
That I may see

The man that shall my husband be,
Not in his best or worst array,
But what he weareth every day;
That I to-morrow may him ken
From among all other men."

On going to bed she must lie on her back, with her hands under her head, and her future spouse will appear in a dream and *salute her with a kiss*.

A BAY LEAF CHARM

On Valentine's Eve (February 13th) take five bay-leaves and pin four of them to the four corners of your pillow and the fifth to the middle. If after doing that you dream of your sweetheart the chances are in favour of your being married before the year is out.

DUMB CAKE

On St. Faith's Eve (October 5th) let three girls who wish to know their fortune in marriage make a cake of flour, spring water, and sugar, each giving an equal hand in the composition. It must be baked in the oven, the strictest silence being observed all the time, lest the spell should be broken, and the cake must be turned thrice by each person. When it is well baked it is to be divided into three equal portions, and each girl must cut her share into nine pieces and draw each piece through a wedding-ring which has been borrowed from a woman who has been married seven years.

Each girl must then eat her pieces of cake, while she is undressing, and repeat the following lines –

"O, good St. Faith, be kind to-night,
  And bring to me my heart's delight;
  Let me my future husband view,
  And be my vision chaste and true."

All three must then get into one bed, with the ring suspended by a string to the head of the bed, and during the night they are certain to dream of their future husbands.

SEEN IN A DREAM

On the eve of St. Luke's Day (the 17th of October) take marigold flowers, a sprig of marjoram, thyme, and a little wormwood; dry them before the fire, rub them to powder, then sift through a fine piece of lawn and simmer over a slow fire, adding a small quantity of honey and vinegar. Anoint yourself with this when you go to bed, saying the following lines three times, and you will dream of your partner that is to be –

"Saint Luke, Saint Luke, be kind to me,
  In dreams let me my true love see."

She must then turn round three times and cast it over her left shoulder. If on falling the paring forms a letter, that is the answer of the oracle; if it breaks, the inquirer may expect to *die an old maid*.

FAITHFUL
OR FAITHLESS?

ASK AN APPLE PIP

To ascertain whether her professing lovers really care for her or not let a girl take an apple pip and, naming one of her followers, put it into the fire. If the pip makes a noise in bursting from the heat, it is a proof of love; but if it is consumed without a crack she may be satisfied that there is no real regard felt towards her by the person named. As many pips should be experimented on as there are lovers.

NAMING NUTS?

If a young woman would know if her lover is faithful she must on All Hallows' Eve put nuts upon the bars of the grate, naming one nut after her lover and one after herself. If the nut representing the lover cracks or jumps the lover will prove unfaithful; if it begins to blaze or burn he has a regard for the person making the trial. If the nuts named after the girl and her lover burn both together they will be married.

VIRTUE IN A CANDLE AND A PIN ◈

Girls who want to know the state of their sweethearts' affections may practise a curious piece of divination with a candle and a pin. She who makes the trial must take a pin and cautiously stick it through the substance of the candle, making sure at the same time that it pierces the wick. Whilst doing so she must repeat the following rhyme –

"It's not this candle alone I stick,
  But A.B.'s heart I mean to prick;
  Whether he be asleep or awake
  I'll have him come to me and speak."

She must then watch the candle as it burns away, and if the pin remains in the wick after the flame has made its way below the place in which it was inserted, she may go to rest with an easy mind, for the loved one will be sure to visit her in dreams. If the pin drops out, however, it is a sign that he is faithless, and not worth thinking about any more.

◈ Important Questions ◈

IS THERE TO BE A WEDDING? ◈

If two forks or knives or spoons are laid down together while setting a table, there is going to be a wedding.

SAVED FROM DYING OLD MAIDS ◈

If in a family the youngest daughter marries before her elder sisters, they should all *dance at her wedding without shoes*; this will counteract their ill-luck and procure them husbands.

HOPE FOR THE UNMARRIED

If, at a dinner, a person yet unmarried be placed inadvertently between a married couple, be sure he or she will get a partner within the year.

WHAT THE WEDDING-CAKE DISCLOSES

In the wedding-cake there should be baked a wedding-ring and a sixpence. When at the wedding breakfast the cake is distributed, she who gets the ring in her portion will shortly be married, and she who gets the sixpence must look upon it as consolation for having to die an old maid. Should they fall to a man's share the ring, of course says, "You will be a married man," but the sixpence, "You will pass your days as a bachelor."

FOR FLIRTS ONLY!

Should a girl find any little stems of tea-leaves in her tea let her swallow them if she wishes to capture a new beau.

IS HE IN GOOD HUMOUR OR BAD?

To test a lover's humour, let a girl lightly stir the fire with the poker. If the fire blazes brightly the lover is good-humoured; if not, he is cross as two sticks.

MAKING SURE OF HIS RETURN ✦

When a lover is going away on a journey, if his best girl will only put common clover into his shoe unknown to him he is sure to return to her.

UNFORTUNATE OMENS ✦

Should you stumble when going up stairs, if you are unmarried you will have no chance of wedding till next year. Should your chair tumble backwards you will certainly not be married during the currency of the present year.

SPELLS FOR MONEY-MAKING

THE GOOSE WITH THE GOLDEN EGGS

If you eat goose on Michaelmas Day you will never want money all the year round.

BY THE AID OF THE MOON

Here is another secret worth knowing. On the first day of the first new moon of the new year, or so soon afterwards as you observe it, all you have to do is this: on the first glance you take at "pale Luna's silvery crest" in the western sky, put your hand in your pocket, shut your eyes, and turn the smallest piece of silver money you possess upside down in your said pocket. This will ensure you (if you will but trust its infallibility) throughout the whole year that summum bonum of earthly wishes, a pocket never empty.

If, however, you neglect on the first appearance of the moon your case is a bad one. Nevertheless and notwithstanding at a future new moon you may pursue the same course, and it will be sure to hold good during the then current month, but not a whit longer.

CHAPTER FOUR

UNDERSTANDING THE SUPERNATURAL

FORTUNES TOLD
BY CARDS

OR the reading of the future there are few methods more popular than the study of the apparently accidental combinations of a pack of cards. By these oracles, many nowadays, as in byegone times, learn their fate and guide their conduct.

The general mode of manipulating the cards, when fortune telling, is very simple. The person who is desirous to know the future, after shuffling the cards *ad libitum*, cuts the pack into three parts.

The seer, then taking up these parts, lays the cards out, one by one, face upwards, upon the table, sometimes in a circular form, but oftener in rows consisting of nine cards in each row. Nine is the mystical number. Every nine consecutive cards form a separate combination complete in itself; yet, like a word in a sentence, no more than a fractional part of the grand scroll of fate. Again, every card, something like the octaves in music, is *en rapport* with the ninth card from it; and these ninth cards form other complete combinations of nines, yet parts of the general whole. The nine of hearts is termed the 'wish-card.'

After the general fortune has been told, a separate and different manipulation is performed, to learn if the pryer into futurity will obtain a particular wish; and, from the position of the wish-card in the pack, the required answer may be deduced.

Here are the interpretations given to the various cards –

❖ DIAMONDS

KING   A man of very fair complexion; quick to anger, but soon appeased.

QUEEN   A very fair woman, fond of gaiety, and a coquette.

KNAVE   A selfish and deceitful relative; fair and false.

TEN   Money. Success in honourable business.

NINE   A roving disposition, combined with honourable and successful adventure in foreign lands.

EIGHT   A happy, prudent marriage, though rather late in life.

SEVEN   Satire. Scandal. Unpleasant business matters.

SIX   Marriage early in life, succeeded by widowhood.

FIVE   Unexpected news, generally of a good kind.

FOUR   An unfaithful friend. A secret betrayed.

TREY   Domestic troubles, quarrels and unhappiness.

DEUCE   A clandestine engagement. A card of caution.

ACE   A wedding ring. An offer of marriage.

⚜ HEARTS

KING A fair, but not very fair, complexioned man; good-natured, but rather obstinate, and, when angered, not easily appeased.

QUEEN A woman of the same complexion as the king; faithful, prudent, and affectionate.

KNAVE An unselfish relative. A sincere friend.

TEN Health and happiness, with many children.

NINE Wealth. High position in society. The wish-card.

EIGHT Fine clothes. Pleasure. Mixing in good society. Going to balls, theatres, &c.

SEVEN Many good friends.

SIX Honourable courtship.

FIVE A present.

FOUR Domestic troubles caused by jealousy.

TREY Poverty, shame, and sorrow, caused by imprudence. A card of caution.

DEUCE Success in life, position in society, and a happy marriage, attained by virtuous discretion.

ACE The house of the person consulting the decrees of fate.

❧ SPADES

KING	A man of very dark complexion, ambitious and unscrupulous.
QUEEN	A very dark-complexioned woman, of malicious disposition. A widow.
KNAVE	A lawyer. A person to be shunned.
TEN	Disgrace; crime; imprisonment. Death on the scaffold. A card of caution.
NINE	Grief; ruin; sickness; death.
EIGHT	Great danger from imprudence. A card of caution.
SEVEN	Unexpected poverty caused by the death of a relative. A lean sorrow.
SIX	A child. To the unmarried a card of caution.
FIVE	Great danger from giving way to bad temper. A card of caution.
FOUR	Sickness.
TREY	A journey by land. Tears.
DEUCE	A removal.
ACE	Death; malice; a duel; a general misfortune.

☀ CLUBS

KING A dark-complexioned man, though not so dark as the king of spades; upright, true, and affectionate.

QUEEN A woman of the same character, agreeable, genteel, and witty.

KNAVE A sincere, but rather hasty-tempered friend.

TEN Unexpected wealth, through the death of a relative. A fat sorrow.

NINE Danger caused by drunkenness. A card of caution.

EIGHT Danger from covetousness. A card of caution.

SEVEN A prison. Danger arising from the opposite sex. A card of caution.

SIX Competence by hard-working industry.

FIVE A happy, though not wealthy marriage.

FOUR Danger of misfortune caused by inconstancy, or capricious temper. A card of caution.

TREY Quarrels. Or in reference to time may signify three years, three months, three weeks, or three days. It also denotes that a person will be married more than once.

DEUCE Vexation, disappointment.

ACE A letter.

THE MYSTERIES
OF SPIRITUALISM

THE mysterious phenomena classed under the name of modern spiritualism have attracted the attention of many distinguished observers, and should be approached by every one with an open mind. There is no doubt that few subjects are more capable of being turned to account by rogues, charlatans, and double-cunning persons, but the fact of anything being abused does not prove it valueless: on the contrary, it suggests that at the bottom of it there is something of real worth and importance. Truth in the long run will prevail about spiritualism as about everything else.

WHAT IS SPIRITUALISM?

Spiritualism, as defined by its supporters, is based on the cardinal fact of spirit communion and influx; it is the effort to *discover all truth relating to man's spiritual nature*, but to those who are mourning over lost friends it assumes an importance of the highest possible character.

WHAT IS A MEDIUM?

Mediums are those who form the links between this world of the living and the world of the dead. Spiritualists are not yet agreed as to the special qualities in mediums which enable spirits to make use of them for communication with the living. It is a well ascertained fact that some at once discover themselves in possession of these special qualities, whilst others who become mediums do so only after prolonged and patient waiting.

EVIDENCE FOR THE SUPERNATURAL

An inquiry into spiritualism was instituted at the close of 1869 by the London Dialectical Society, who appointed a committee "to investigate the phenomena alleged to be spiritual manifestations, and to report thereon."

And what was the result? After a careful and prolonged investigation, the committee reported in July, 1871, that a "large majority" of its members "have become actual witnesses to several phases of the phenomena, without the aid or

presence of any professional medium, although the greater part of them commenced their investigations in an avowedly sceptical spirit."

Here is their synopsis of the evidence laid before them –

❧ **THIRTEEN WITNESSES STATE** that they have seen heavy *bodies* – in some instances men *rise slowly in the air*, and remain there for some time without visible or tangible support.

❧ **FIVE WITNESSES STATE** that they have been *touched by some invisible agency* on various parts of the body, and often where requested, when the hands of all present were visible.

❧ **EIGHT WITNESSES STATE** that they have received detailed *information through rappings, writings*, or in other ways, the accuracy of which was unknown at the time to themselves or to any persons present, and which on subsequent inquiry was found to be correct.

❧ **THIRTEEN WITNESSES DECLARE** that they have *heard musical pieces* well played upon instruments not manipulated by any ascertainable agency.

SIX WITNESSES DECLARE that they have *received information of future events*, and that in some cases the hour and minute have been accurately foretold days and even weeks before.

In addition to the above evidence was given before the committee of trance-speaking, of healing, of automatic writing, of the introduction of flowers and fruits into closed rooms, of voices in the air, of visions in crystals and glasses, and of the elongation of the human body.

COMMUNICATION WITH
THE OTHER SIDE

TABLE-TURNING

The phenomenon of spiritualism which attracted most attention when the spiritualistic movement first spread from the New to the Old World in 1852, was table-turning. There was a positive mania for table-turning all over Europe in the following year.

We must choose in preference to others a *wooden table* without marble, standing on castors well oiled, or turning easily on its stand. To relieve the tedium of waiting, the experimenters should be of different sexes, in nearly equal proportions, and placed alternately. Placed in this manner, whether sitting or standing, the experimenters will lay their hands, spread out on the table in an easy position with the palm downwards, and will put them in contact with their neighbour's by means of their little fingers.

When the table begins to move it must be followed quickly by the experimenters, care being taken not to break the chain, in which case the movement would immediately cease. But the chain should be again formed immediately.

TO MAKE THE TABLE SPEAK

In conducting a spiritualistic circle, at which the table is made to speak and answer questions put to it, or rather put to the intelligence controlling it, two or three conditions besides those already named should be observed.

The room should be moderately warm, while the parties who are to sit should – in order to secure harmony – be passive and serious, endeavouring, as far as possible, to lay aside preconceived notions and allow the facts to speak for themselves.

After the experimenters have sat quiet for some time – perhaps for fifteen to thirty minutes – some will feel their hands begin to grow cold, while those of the others will remain warm, or perhaps grow warmer. It is advisable, then, to place those whose hands are cold opposite those whose hands are warm. At this stage the gas may be lowered in order to intensify the magnetic conditions that have thus been established.

When the experiment arrives at the point of success instead of movements the party may get slight explosive cracks from the table, which gradually increase to distinct raps. But whether raps or movements it will now be time to put questions to the intelligence moving the table.

The first question should be whether it will reply to questions put to it by giving one rap or movement for "yes", three for "no", and two for "doubtful". By this mode you can obtain answers to all questions requiring a negative or affirmative reply.

For longer communication you must use the alphabet. Having ascertained the spirit's willingness to do so, you begin at A, repeating the letters distinctly, till you arrive at the required letter, which will be indicated by a rap or movement of the table; you then repeat the process, and in this way form words and sentences. This process is both tedious and uncertain, to obviate which some use what is called an indicator; but even this is open to the same objections. But on this subject the reader may turn to what we have said in a preceding section.

Mystery and Danger
~ in Hypnotism ~

RELATED TO MESMERISM ~

Spiritualism has a close connection with mesmerism. Indeed, spiritualists say that the difference between them just lies in this, that in the case of mesmerism the operator is a mortal being, whereas in spiritualism the operator is a disembodied human spirit, with a spiritual body instead of one of flesh and blood.

This subject is not to be lightly dealt with, and not at all to be experimented in except by those prepared to treat it in a serious, inquiring, and scientific spirit.

By means of mesmerism or hypnotism – you may call it which you please – the mind and body of an individual are influenced by a mysterious power proceeding from another person, and "most thinking people," it has been well said, "will hesitate before they run the risk of submitting themselves to an influence which may end in the surrender of their will to another, the annihilation of their very identity."

HOW TO PRODUCE THE MESMERIC STATE

From a well-informed writer in the *Popular Science Monthly* –

"With one hand, a bright object, such as a faceted piece of glass, is held eight to twelve inches from the subject, so that there is considerable convergence of the eyes, and rather above the level of the eyes, so that he is obliged to look upward. The subject is told to look steadily at the piece of glass, and to keep his whole attention fixed upon it.

"This position is kept up for five or ten minutes; during this time the pupils will probably dilate considerably; when this is the case the free hand is moved slowly from the object towards the eyes. If the subject is sensitive, the eyes will usually close with a vibratory motion. In some cases the subject is then unable to open them, and the usual mesmeric phenomena can be obtained.

"If, when the operator brings his hand near the eyes of the subject, the subject instead of closing them follows the movements of the fingers, the whole proceeding is repeated. When the subject is inclined to pass into the cataleptic state, an indication of his condition may be obtained by gently raising his arm; if he is beginning to be mesmerised, the arm remains in the position in which it is placed. If the arm falls, the mesmeric state may not infrequently be hastened on by telling the subject to keep his arm extended while he is still gazing at the object. And that is the whole of the process."

WHEN IN THE HYPNOTIC STATE

When in his sleep-like condition the subject may be made to make movements as directed by the operator, and to act in accordance with ideas suggested to him. "Thus he may *eat a raw onion* with gusto, apparently under the impression that it is an apple; he may make wry faces on drinking a glass of water when told that what he is taking is castor oil; he may ride on a chair or stool as in a horse race; he may *fight with imaginary enemies* or show tokens of affection to imaginary friends; in short, all kinds of actions, even of a ridiculous and degrading nature, may be done by the subject at the command of the operator."

HOW TO BRING ONE OUT OF
THE HYPNOTIC STATE

To bring the person in the hypnotic state out of it again, it is only necessary to blow lightly on the face and say "Wake up!" If left to themselves subjects eventually return to the normal state sooner or later.

SECOND-SIGHT

ECOND-SIGHT is not something to be acquired, and no rules can be given for it. It is a power which is born with the possessor. It is a singular faculty "of seeing an otherwise invisible object, and without any previous means used by the person that beholds it for that end." Some people disbelieve it, but according to Sir Walter Scott, "if force of evidence could authorise us to believe facts inconsistent with the general laws of nature, enough might be produced in favour of the existence of the second-sight."

IN THE HIGHLANDS

A great haunt of the second-sighted was long the highlands and islands of Scotland, and it was there they were made the subject of very careful inquiry by the famous Dr. Samuel Johnson. "Second-sight," he says, "is an impression made either upon the eye or by the eye upon the mind, by which things distant or future are perceived, and seen as if they were present. A man on a journey, far from home, falls from his horse; another, who is perhaps at work about the house, sees him bleeding on the ground, commonly with a landscape of the place where the accident befalls him. Another seer, driving home his cattle, or wandering in idleness, or musing in the sunshine, is suddenly surprised by the appearance of a bridal ceremony, or a funeral procession, and counts the mourners or attendants, of whom, if he knows them, he relates the names; if he knows them not he can describe their dresses. Things distant are seen at the instant when they happen."

THINGS SEEN BY SECOND-SIGHT ✦

Of things future, the rules of interpretation are numerous. If a vision occurs by day, for example, the accomplishment of what it predicts will be speedy; if by night, less so. An exact proportion, indeed, is maintained in this respect – the morning vision being sooner fulfilled than that of noon; the latter more quickly than that of the afternoon, and so on.

✦ FIGURE IN A SHROUD

If the seer beholds a figure in a shroud, it is a sure sign of death to the party represented by the figure; and according to the extent to which the shroud covers the body, the end will be quicker or slower.

AN EMPTY SEAT

To see a seat as if vacant when one is sitting in it, is a presage of the party's death.

A WOMAN

If a woman be seen at a man's left hand, it is a presage that she will be his wife, and this will be the case even though both should then be married.

If more than one woman be seen standing at a man's left hand they will be married to him in rotation, as they stand nearer or farther from his arm.

A VISITOR

A seer often announces that such and such a guest will arrive at a certain hour; and though a hundred miles away when that is told, the guest will appear at the stated time.

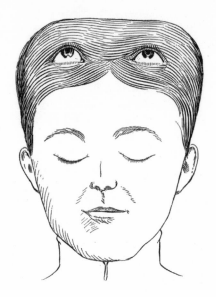

❧ TREES AND HOUSES

If a seer observes a vision of trees and crops in some spot or other, though perfectly barren and bare at the moment, wood and grain will be seen there in due time. A visionary house is beheld by the gifted eye, in a place where stone and lime were never laid or expected to be laid. Yet there will the real house forthwith be seen.

❧ INSTANCES OF SECOND-SIGHT

There are many instances of second-sight recorded in history. According to a well-known anecdote, "St. Ambrose fell into a comatose state while celebrating the Mass at Milan, and on his recovery declared that he had been present at St. Martin's funeral at Tours, where, indeed, reports from Tours afterwards declared that he had been seen."

In modern times the gift of second-sight was possessed in a remarkable degree by Emanuel Swedenborg, the founder of the New Church. The following is a well-authenticated instance. Once while taking supper at Gottenburg, at the house of William Castel, on the 10th of July, 1759, Swedenborg became excited. "He said," we quote from a letter written by the celebrated philosopher Kant, "that a dangerous fire had broken out in Stockholm, at the Suderhalm (Stockholm is about three hundred miles from Gottenburg), and that it was spreading very fast.

"He was restless and went out often; he said that the house of one of his friends, whom he named, was already in ashes, and that his own was in danger. At eight o'clock, after he had been out again, he joyfully exclaimed, 'Thank God! the fire is extinguished the third door from my house.' "

As may readily be supposed, this created a great deal of talk in Gottenburg. Three days afterwards the news of the fire arrived in that city by royal courier, and Swedenborg's statement was confirmed in every particular.

A Scottish seer is said to have foretold the unhappy career of Charles; and another predicted the violent end of Villiers, Duke of Buckingham.

CHAPTER FIVE

BEINGS FROM OTHER WORLDS

FAIRY FOLK

THE characters of different classes of spirits have become so mingled together in the lapse of time that it is difficult to define individual species with precision; but there is one key characteristic which distinguishes the fairy from every other being of a similar order.

Most spirits can contract and diminish their bulk at will, but the fairy alone is essentially small in size. The majority of other spirits also, such as dwarfs, brownies, and the like, are deformed creatures, whereas the fairy is a *beautiful miniature of the human being*, perfect in face and form. These points of distinction, with a dress of pure green, are the principal ones, which mark the personal individuality of the fairies as a supernatural race.

THE LAND OF FAERIE ❖

This is situated somewhere underground, and there the royal fairies hold their court. In their palaces all is beauty and splendour. Their pageants and processions are far more magnificent than any that Eastern sovereigns could get up or poets devise. They ride upon milk-white steeds. Their dresses, of brilliant green, are rich beyond conception; and when they mingle in the dance, or move in procession among the shady groves, or over the verdant lawns of earth, they are entertained with delicious music, such as mortal lips or hands never could emit or produce.

REALM OF THE FAIRIES ❖

The presence of grass growing undisturbed by man is the spell which preserves the plain and the hillside as the domain of the fairies and other invisible people. Once it is ploughed up the spell is gone and they change their abode. "Where the scythe cuts, and the sock rives," says an old Scottish proverb, "hae done wi' fairies and bee bykes!" (nests of wild bees).

FAIRY RINGS

What are known as fairy rings are formed by the feet of the fairies as they dance in the great hall of nature, whose dome is the midnight sky. The grass, out of sympathy with their merriment, grows greener and more luxuriant under their tread.

To plough up these fairy rings is not lucky. There is a Scottish rhyme which says –

"He wha tills the fairies' green,
 Nae luck again shall hae;
 And he who spills the fairies' ring,
 Betide him want and wae;
 For weirdless days and weary nights
 Are his, till his deein' day."

There is another Scottish rhyme much to the same purpose and containing a promise to any kind soul who will keep the ring trim and neat –

"He wha goes by the fairies' ring,
 Nae dule nor pine shall see;
 And he wha cleans the fairies' ring,
 An easy death shall dee."

The neighbourhood of fairy rings is lucky ground. If a house is built on ground where they are, "whoever shall inhabit therein shall prosper considerably."

THE POWERS OF CHILDREN

CHILDREN are under the special guardianship of those who reside in the other world. Their start in life and their ultimate success or failure depends on a great deal over which their parents have no control.

THE POWER OF SEEING SPIRITS

A child who has come into the world during twilight has in after life the power of seeing spirits, and is gifted to know who of his circle of acquaintance will die next.

The gift of second sight also belongs to a child born on All Saints' Eve and on Christmas Day.

IN DANGER OF FAIRY SPELLS

A newborn child is in danger of fairy spells till it sneezes: then all danger is past.

"UNCHRISTENED WEANS."

Unchristened children are peculiarly liable to be carried off by the fairies, who sometimes *leave little changelings*, of their own blood, in place of the infants of mortal kind.

PREPARED FOR RISING IN THE WORLD

When children first leave their mother's room they must go upstairs before they go downstairs, otherwise they will never rise in the world.

Of course it frequently happens that there is no "upstairs," the mother's room being the highest in the house. In this case the difficulty is met by the nurse setting a chair and stepping upon that with the child in her arms as she leaves the room.

MOTHERS SHOULD OBSERVE THESE THINGS

- A baby laughing in its dreams is conversing with the angels.
- Children with much down on their hands or arms are sure to be rich.
- When the teeth of a child come early it is an indication that there will soon be another baby.
- If a child's first tooth is in the upper jaw it is ominous of its dying in infancy.
- To cut a child's nails before it is twelve months old is unlucky.
- Rocking the cradle when the babe is not in it is injurious to the infant, and a prognostic of its speedy death.

WHAT ABOUT WITCHES?

"Witches can blight our corn by magic spell,
 And with enchantments dry the springing well."
 – OVID.

THE POWERS OF WITCHES

An old writer, speaking of the powers of witches, says –

"1. Some work their bewitchings only by way of invocation or imprecation. They wish it, or will it; and so it falls out.

"2. Some, by way of emissary, sending out their imps, or familiars, to crosse the way, justle, affront, flash in the face, barke, howle, bite, scratch, or otherwise infest.

"3. Some by inspecting, or looking on, or to glare, or to peep at with an envious and evil eye.

"4. Some by a hollow muttering or mumbling.

"5. Some by breathing and blowing on.

"6. Some by cursing and banning.

"7. Some by blessing and praising.

"8. Some revengefully, by occasion of ill turnes.

"9. Some ingratefully, and by reason of good turnes.

"10. Some by leaving something of theirs in your house.

"11. Some by getting something of yours into their house.

"12. Some have a more speciall way of working by severall elements – earth, water, ayre, or fire. But who can tell all the manner of wayes of a witch's working; that works not only darkly and closely, but variously and versatilly, as God will permit, the devil can suggest, or the malicious hag devise to put in practice?"

THE WITCH'S ATTENDANTS

The *toad* and the *black cat* are the most usual attendants of the witch, or rather the form her imps most commonly assume.

HOW TO SEE WITCHES

Grass is useful for enabling us to see witches when by their arts they make themselves invisible. Whoever wants to do so, let him place himself in a cross-way on May-night or on St. John's eve, *cut a piece of turf and lay it on his head*. Under these conditions, the witches can do him no harm; they will be visible to him but he will be unseen by them.

For seeing witches rye is also of service. The only thing necessary is to gather rye from three fields and carry it in the pocket.

CHURCH BELLS

Church bells are very useful for dispersing by their sacred peals the tempests raised by the power of witches.

WITCHES IN PURSUIT

"Neither witches nor any evil spirits," says Robert Burns, "have power to follow a poor wight any further than the middle of the next running stream." We all know the use the poet makes of this fact in his famous poem of "Tam o' Shanter" –

> "Now, do thy speedy utmost, Meg,
> And win the keystone o' the brig;
> There at them thou thy tail may toss,
> A running stream they darena cross."

THE SIGN OF THE CROSS

This holy sign keeps witches and all evil spirits at a distance. To them it is a hated symbol near which they will not voluntarily approach. If anything seems in danger through their wicked wiles, make the sign of the cross over it and it is safe.

HORSESHOES AGAINST WITCHES

A horseshoe hung up behind the door is a means of securing good luck to the household and protecting it from witchcraft and from the influence of the evil eye.

Mrs. Coutts, who afterwards became the Duchess of St. Albans, was a great believer in the power of the horseshoe. The steps at Holly Lodge were composed of beautiful blocks of white marble which a statuary might envy, and on the highest step were two rusty old broken horseshoes fastened, which Mrs. Coutts and her husband had found in the road.

These pieces of rusty iron they had nailed on the threshold of their home to avert evil and bring good luck.

The luckiest horseshoes and those which give the most powerful protection are *those which are found*, not bought ones.

Nelson, we may mention, had a horseshoe nailed to the mast of the *Victory*.

FLYING THROUGH THE AIR NOT ILLEGAL

Lord Mansfield had an old woman brought before him as a witch, and among other things she was charged with riding through the air. The great judge dismissed the case, observing, "My opinion is that this good woman should be suffered to return home, and whether she do so by walking on the ground or riding through the air must be left to her own judgment; for there is nothing contrary to the laws of England in either."

WITCHES CHANGE THEIR SHAPE

Witches have the power of *changing their shape* and resuming it again at will. In illustration of this we may quote the following incident that occurred in the neighbourhood of a village in Cornwall. A large hare, which haunted the district, had on numberless occasions baffled the hounds, or carried off, unhurt, incredible quantities of shot. One luckless day it crossed the path of a party of determined sportsmen, who followed it for many weary miles, and fired several rounds, with the usual want of success. Before relinquishing the chase, one of them, who considered the animal as something beyond an ordinary hare, suggested the trial of silver bullets, and, accordingly, silver coins were beaten into slugs for this purpose. The hare was again seen, fired at, and this time wounded, though not so effectually as to prevent its running round the brow of the hill, and disappearing among the rocks. In searching for the hare, they discovered instead old Molly, crouched under a shelving rock, panting and flushed by the long chase. From that day forward she had a limp in her gait.

CHAPTER SIX

WHAT WE MAY LEARN FROM THE BODY

LOOKS SHOW YOUR CHARACTER

ONE may certainly read the characters of men and form an accurate estimate of what they are by studying their general appearance, and particularly their faces. We need the help which it supplies to enable us to distinguish between fit companions and unfit, trustworthy customers and untrustworthy, rogues and honest men, wise folk and simpletons.

A GOOD GENERAL RULE

If the first moment in which a person appears in a proper light be entirely advantageous for him; if his first impression have in it nothing repulsive or oppressive, and produce in you no kind of restraint; he will always, so long as no person intervenes between you, gain upon you and never lose. Nature has formed you for each other.

NOT ALWAYS PLEASING AT FIRST SIGHT

Take notice, however, that some countenances gain greatly upon us the more they are known, though they do not please at the first moment.

UNCHANGING FACES

When people have countenances that never conspicuously change, they are very discreet, or very cold, or very dull.

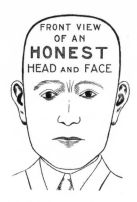

FRONT VIEW
OF AN
HONEST
HEAD AND FACE

NOT AT ALL STRAIGHT ✦

Of any one whose figure is oblique, whose mouth is oblique, whose walk is oblique, whose hand-writing is oblique – that is, in an unequal, irregular direction – we may infer that his manner of thinking, character, and conduct are oblique, inconsistent, partial, false, sly, crafty, whimsical, contradictory, and wanting in sensibility.

THE FOREHEAD ✦

✦ DIGNIFIED WRINKLES

When a finely arched forehead has in the middle, between the eyebrows, a slightly discernible, perpendicular, not too long wrinkle or two parallel wrinkles of that kind – especially when the eyebrows are marked, compressed, and regular – it is to be ranked among the foreheads of the first magnitude. Such foreheads, beyond all doubt, belong only to wise and masculine mature characters; and when they are found in women it is difficult to find any more discreet and sensible, more betokening royal dignity and propriety of manners.

CRUEL EYES

✤ A WEAK INTELLECT

That forehead betokens weakness of intellect which has in the middle and lower part a scarcely observable long cavity. Every forehead which above projects, and below sinks in towards the eye, in a person of mature age is a certain sign of incurable imbecility. The fewer hollows, arches, and indentations, the more is that forehead common, mediocre, destitute of ideas, and incapable of invention.

✤ SMALL, BLACK, SPARKLING EYES

These, under strong black eyebrows – deep sunken in jesting laughter, are seldom destitute of cunning, penetration, and artful simulation. If they are unaccompanied by a jesting mouth, they denote cool reflection, taste, elegance, accuracy, and an inclination rather to avarice than generosity.

Eyes which, in the moment when they are fixed on the most sacred object of their adoration, express no veneration and inspire no seriousness and reverence, can never make claim to beauty, nor sensibility, nor spirituality. Trust them not. They cannot love or be loved. No lineament of the countenance full of truth and power can be found with them.

✤ OF WHAT COLOUR ARE THE EYES?

✤ Black eyes are usually a sign of good powers of physical endurance; but they are choleric, and may be, though they are not always, treacherous.

- Grey eyes indicate a quick temper, coolness in the presence of danger, and a love of novelty.
- Those with grey eyes are generally keen, energetic, and at first cold; but you may rely upon their sympathy with real sorrow.
- Hazel eyes are found with shrewd people, and such as take pleasure in intercourse with friends.
- A calm blue eye well enclosed by the eyebrows shows a good judge of character.
- Clear blue eyes are associated with love of change and progress.

We add a companion rhyme often repeated to young girls –

"Brown eyes – beauty,
Do your mother's duty.
Blue eyes – pick-a-pie,
Lie abed and tell a lie.
Grey eyes – greediness,
Gobble all the world up."

DECEITFUL EYE

HONEST EYE

⚘ DROOPING EYELIDS

A drooping of the upper eyelids is not a good sign; it is generally observed in persons of low, cunning disposition and very secretive habits.

⚘ NO WRINKLES

Eyes which discover no wrinkles when they appear amorous, always appertain only to little, feeble characters, or even betoken total imbecility.

THE EYEBROWS TELL THEIR TALE ≈

≈ **HORIZONTAL EYEBROWS**, rich and clear, always denote understanding, coldness of heart, and capacity for framing plans. Wild eyebrows are never found with a mild, ductile, pliable character.

≈ **THICK, BLACK, STRONG EYEBROWS**, which decline downwards and appear to lie close upon the eye, are only to be consulted for advice when revenge is sought, or the brutal desire of doing injury to others is entertained – in other respects they are to be treated in as yielding a manner as possible, and that yielding as much as possible concealed.

≈ **HEAVY EYEBROWS** denote a strong character; light ones indicate a weak or flippant temperament. If the brows are straight and-square they show a direct and earnest character. If they have an uncertain curve you may infer a wavering disposition.

≈ **A CLEAR, THICK, ROOF-SHAPED**, overshadowing eyebrow, which has no wild luxuriant bushiness, is always a sign of a sound, manly, mature understanding.

≈ **THE EYEBROW WITH A BEAUTIFUL CURVE** and graduated ending belongs to persons of an imaginative and amiable disposition. Should the eyebrows turn upwards at the ends the person is of an inquiring turn of mind.

THESE WHO FROWN under overhanging eyebrows are eccentric and penurious; the broad, smooth eyebrow betokens meditation, and that with the raised tuft in the middle, humour.

NOTES ON NOSES

A nose is the sum of the forehead and the root of the underpart of the countenance.

NOSES WHICH ARE MUCH TURNED DOWNWARDS are never truly good. When arched in the upper part they are fearful and voluptuous.

NOSES WHICH ARE SOMEWHAT TURNED UP at the point are by nature inclined to pleasure, ease, jealousy, pertinacity.

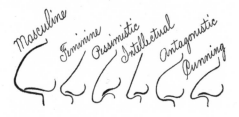

Masculine   Feminine   Pessimistic   Intellectual   Antagonistic   Cunning

NOSES WITHOUT ANY REMARKABLE CHARACTER may indeed be found with rational, good, and occasionally in some degree superior characters; but never with such as are truly great and excellent.

NOSES WHICH EASILY AND CONTINUALLY TURN UP in wrinkles are seldom to be found in truly good men, as those which will seldom wrinkle, even with an effort, are in men *consummately wicked*.

✧ **WHEN NOSES WHICH NOT ONLY EASILY WRINKLE**, but have the traces of these wrinkles indented in them, are found in good men, these good, well-disposed men are half fools.

✧ **NOSES OF CONSIDERABLE SIZE**. A person with a long nose has, as a rule, also a marked and forcible character. It has been said indeed that Nature provides men with long noses that she may have a good handle to lay hold of when she wants to pull them to the front.

THE MOUTH ✧

✧ **EVERY MOUTH WHICH IS FULL** as broad again as the eye, that is, from the corner towards the nose to the internal end of the eye, both measured with the same rectilinear measure, denotes dullness or stupidity.

✧ **THE WISEST AND BEST MEN** have well-proportioned upper and under lips.

✧ **LARGE, WELL-PROPORTIONED LIPS** always denote a sensual, indelicate, and sometimes a wicked man.

✧ **HE, THE ENDS OF WHOSE LIPS SINK** conspicuously and obliquely downwards, has contempt on his lips and is devoid of love in his heart – especially when the under lip is larger and more projecting than the upper.

Impulsive Lips.

CHARACTER IN THE CHIN ❧

A long, broad, thick chin – we speak of the bony chin – is only found in rude, harsh, proud, and violent persons.

CHARACTER IN THE HAIR ❧

❧ **LONG-HAIRED MEN** are generally weak and fanatical, and men with scanty locks are the philosophers and soldiers and statesmen of the world.

❧ **ABUNDANT HAIR** is neither an indication of bodily nor of mental strength. The easily wheedled Esau was hairy; the mighty Cæsar was bald.

❧ **RED HAIR**, according to Lavater, characterises a man singularly good or singularly bad, and, he adds, "a striking contrast between the colour of the hair and the colour of the eyebrows inspires me with disgust."

THE COLOUR OF THE MOUSTACHE

This indicates character. According to an Italian writer, a black moustache shows a manly boldness; brown, a hot head and good temper; red, wiliness; blonde, a noble soul; white, a lack of vital heat; bristly, fury; thick, rusticity; coarse, audacity; and scanty, languor.

OBSTINATE PEOPLE

The higher the forehead and the less the remainder of the countenance appears in consequence, the more knotty the concave forehead, the deeper sunken the eye, the less excavation there is between the forehead and the nose, the more closed the mouth, the broader the chin, the more perpendicular the long profile of the countenance, the more unyielding the obstinacy, the harsher the character.

EARS SHOW CHARACTER

According to Aristotle, large ears indicate imbecility, while small ones announce madness. Flat ears point out rustic and brutal people. Those that promise best are firm and middling-sized ears. That man is happy who boasts of square ears – a sure indication of sublimity of soul and purity of life.

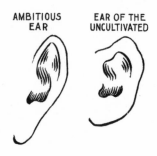

AMBITIOUS   EAR OF THE
EAR   UNCULTIVATED

FORWARD WOMAN

No forward, confident woman is formed for friendship. Such a character no woman can conceal, however prudent or artful she may be. Observe only the sides of the nose and the upper lip, in profile, when mention is made of another woman, whether a rival or not a rival, who excites attention.

A BAD SIGN

A *broad brown wart* on the chin is never found in truly wise, noble persons, but very frequently in such as are remarkable for imbecility. When it is found in the countenance of a man of sense we may be certain of frequent intervals of the most extreme thoughtlessness, absence of mind, and feebleness of intellect.

WORTHLESS INSIGNIFICANCE

Puffed, withered cheeks, a large swollen mouth; a middling or rather small figure; freckles in the face; weak, straight hair; forbidding, interrupted wrinkles in the forehead; a skull with a steep descent towards the forehead; eyes which never survey an object naturally and tranquilly, and of which the corners turn upwards – form together a receipt for a *character of worthless insignificance.*

123

THE SMILE

He who gains on you in a smile and loses in a laugh – who, without smiling, appears to smile condescendingly and when silent conciliates him all around him – who, when he smiles or laughs at what is witty or humorous, betrays no cold contemning derision – who smiles with pleasure when he observes the joys of innocence or hears the praise of virtue – will have in his physiognomy and his character everything noble, everything harmonising.

PEOPLE TO BE AVOIDED

Be as circumspect as possible in the presence of a corpulent, choleric man who continually speaks loud, is never at his ease, and looks round with rolling eyes; who has accustomed himself to the external parade of politeness and ceremony, and who does everything with slovenliness and without order. In his round, short, snubbed nose, in his open mouth, his projecting protuberance-producing forehead, his sounding step, are contempt and harshness – half-qualities with pretension to super-eminence, malignity with the external appearance of civility and good-humour.

A GENUINE HUSBAND

AN UNRELIABLE HUSBAND

DISCORDANT CHARACTERS

If you have a long, high forehead contract no friendship with an almost spherical head; if you have an almost spherical head contract no friendship with a long, high, bony forehead. Such dissimilarity is especially unsuitable to matrimony.

PALMISTRY

MANY people regard palmistry as mere guess-work. This it is not. It is claimed by its professors as an exact science founded on careful observation. Much has been said against it, but it is as ancient as the science of medicine, which also in earlier times had its facts disputed.

GENERAL DIRECTIONS

Each line, mark, or sign may be read by itself, but the student of this wonderful science must not imagine that he will thereby get a correct reading of the character. The signs must be taken as a whole, for one sign aids in the interpretation of another. For example, in a fairly good hand we may meet with a bad sign: now that bad sign would be greatly modified by the good signs.

A HINT TO STUDENTS

Before you confidently draw a bad inference be sure you have found the unfavourable sign clearly marked in both hands.

The first thing the student should take note of is the *shape of the hands and fingers*, together with the *skin and nails*. These all relate to the hereditary influences of character and disposition. Next he must give his attention to the mounts, lines and markings which record past and present events and, it may be, reveal the future.

By preference reliance is to be placed on the markings of the left hand, but the right hand is to be consulted for corroborative evidence.

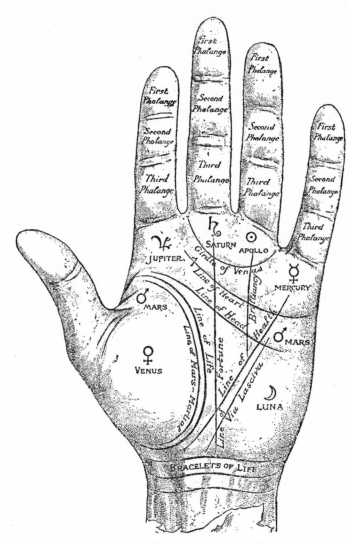

THE MAP OF THE HAND.

THUMB AND FINGERS

The thumb and fingers are each divided by the joints into three phalanges. In the first of these, that nearest the tip of the finger, we have the intuitive faculties represented; in the second, the middle one, we have the reasoning powers; in the third, that nearest the hand, the material instincts are to be found.

THE MOUNTS

- The fingers are named (starting with the forefinger), Jupiter, Saturn, Apollo, and Mercury, and the fleshy pads found at the base of each finger are known as the Mount of Jupiter, Mount of Saturn, and so on.
- The third phalange, or "Ball" of the thumb, gets the name of the Mount of Venus.
- There is a Mount of Mars below the Mount of Jupiter, and another below the Mount of Mercury.
- Extending from the last-named mount up to the wrist is the Mount of Luna, or the Moon.
- On the centre of the palm is the Plain or Triangle of Mars.

Here is what we find denoted by the different Mounts –
JUPITER denotes ambition, pride, self-respect, &c.
SATURN – Caution or prudence, sadness, doubting, &c.
APOLLO – Love of art and genius, celebrity.
MERCURY – Science and industry, speculation, conceit, cheerfulness, &c.

VENUS – Love of pleasure, love of music, love of beauty, and the company of the opposite sex.

MARS (beneath Jupiter) – Courage, control, warlike spirit.

MARS (beneath Mercury) – Resistance, command, resignation, anger.

MOON (Luna) – Imagination.

THE LINES

The leading lines of the palm with their characteristics are as follows –

THE LINE OF LIFE – This should begin near the Mount of Jupiter, and run round the base of the thumb towards the wrist. If perfect it should completely encircle the Mount of Venus. A long, regular line, deep but narrow, and soft in colour, is an evidence of long, healthy life and a good character. On it may be read the actions of life and its changes.

THE LINE OF MARS is an inner or sister line to the Line of Life. In soldiers it denotes success in warfare; in civilians violence in their passions.

THE LINE OF THE HEAD – This starts from the Mount of Jupiter, near the beginning of the Line of Life, and runs across the palm to the Mount of Mars. If even, narrow and long it shows strong will and judgment and acute mental perception. The intellectual force is more or less according to the development of the line.

THE LINE OF FORTUNE, OR FATE, OR SUCCESS – This line should run in an unbroken line from the wrist or "Bracelet" to the base of the second finger. The general direction often varies. Success or good fortune depends on the condition of this line. Observations should be taken from both the right hand and the left when drawing inferences from the Line of Fate.

THE LINE OF THE HEART runs from the Mount of Jupiter, at the base of the forefinger, to the Mount of Mercury, at the base of the Mount of Mercury. In this line we get a knowledge of the affections. If deep, of a good colour and narrow, it shows a strong good heart, lasting affection and even temper. Should the heart line be more strongly developed than the head line, we may safely infer that the person will be governed by the heart rather than by the head, but it will be the other way if the head line is the more marked.

THE LINE OF APOLLO OR BRILLIANCY – This line runs parallel to the Line of Fortune and terminates at the base of the third finger. Those who possess it are fortunate. It stands for fame in the arts.

THE LINE OF HEALTH starts diagonally from the wrist and goes to meet the Line of the Head close to the Mount of Mars or at the top of the Mount of Luna. In many hands it is wanting.

THE GIRDLE OF VENUS below the Mounts of Saturn and Apollo is often absent, which is not to be regretted, as it is, on the whole, a mark of a character to be avoided.

THE VIA LASCIVA (Milky Way) runs from the wrist parallel to the Line of Health across the Mount of Luna. It is sometimes mistaken for the Line of Health. It is a sign of a faithless and cunning spirit.

THE BRACELETS OF LIFE are found encircling the wrist. They indicate long life, fortune, and happiness. According to some chiromancers they indicate each thirty years of life.

The palm reveals its secrets through the varying condition of the lines and mounts; careful observation must also be made on the general shape and aspect of the whole hand. Every joint of each finger on each hand is dedicated to and is under the protection of some saint or celestial being.

RIGHT HAND

The top joint of the thumb is dedicated to God; the second joint to the Virgin; the top joint of the forefinger to Bärnabas, the second joint to John, the third joint to Paul; the top joint of the second finger to Simeon Cleophas, the second joint to St. Catharine, the third to Joseph; the top joint of the third finger to Zaccheus, the second to Stephen, the third to Luke; the top joint of the little finger to St. Christopher, the second to Mark, the third joint to Nicodemus.

LEFT HAND

The top joint of the thumb is dedicated to Christ, the second joint to the Virgin; the top joint of the forefinger to St. James, the second to St. John the Evangelist, the third to St. Peter; the first joint of the second finger to St. Simeon, the second joint to St. Matthew, the third to St. James the Great; the top joint of the third finger to St. Jude, the second joint to St. Bartholomew, the third to St. Andrew, and the top joint of the little finger to St. Mathias, the second joint to St. Thomas, the third joint to St. Philip.

CHARACTER JUDGED BY HANDS AND FINGERS

DIFFERENCES OF HANDS

The differences of hands, according to age and sex, are very significant. The woman's hand, independently of the effects of different occupations, is naturally smaller, narrower, softer, less hairy, and more delicate than the man's, and the fingers are more roundly formed.

When these characters are reversed, they mark as clearly as any other misplaced features do the similarly displaced mind: they betray the strong-minded woman and the effeminate man.

THREE TYPES OF HANDS

Hands are divided into three types: the pointed-fingered, or *spiritual*; the square-fingered, or *intellectual*; and the spade-shaped, or *material*. Points, squares, and spades refer to the tips of the fingers.

POINTED FINGER-TIPS

These go with poetry, art in its highest forms, religion, heroism, quickness of body and mind, rapid intuitions, strong likes and dislikes, gifts of imagination, impulsiveness, and many other kindred qualities.

SQUARE HANDS

Intellect, practical gifts, power to plod on unflaggingly, success in life, often belong to square hands – that is to say, to square finger-tips.

SPADE-SHAPED TIPS

Stamp the type as material. A little pad of flesh sticks out at each side of the nail, and the fingers look as if they had been chopped off by some sharp instrument. This is the hand of the sons of toil.

AN IMPORTANT FINGER

The thumb is by far the most important part of the hand. Here we look for the great controlling powers, will and logic. A small, ill-formed, feeble, badly balanced thumb indicates a vacillating disposition. Small-thumbed persons are governed by the heart, while the large-thumbed are ruled by the head. Independent, self-reliant people have large thumbs, or ought to have them, while pliant, dependent, and easily governed natures may be known by the marked smallness of that digit.

OBSERVATIONS ON THE FINGER-NAILS ≈

The dispositions of people may be made out by observing their finger-nails.

BROAD NAILS indicate a gentle nature, timid and bashful.

IF THE NAILS GROW INTO THE FLESH at the joints or sides it is a sign of a desire for luxury.

A WHITE MARK on the nails bespeaks misfortune.

PALE NAILS show people of a weak disposition, subject to persecution by neighbours and friends.

NARROW NAILS belong to ambitious and quarrelsome people.

ROUND NAILS indicate lovers of knowledge and persons of liberal sentiments.

FLESHY NAILS usually show indolent people.

SMALL NAILS are characteristic of small-minded, obstinate, and conceited people.

RED AND SPOTTED NAILS show choleric people, delighting in making a disturbance.

CHARACTER SHOWN
BY HANDWRITING

T is a generally acknowledged fact that the leading points of a person's character can be ascertained from his or her handwriting; indeed, the reading of character by handwriting has in these days become almost a regular profession.

A REASON FOR DIFFERENCES OF HANDWRITING

There is a physiological reason, no doubt, for diversities of handwriting, and that is, temperament. "Let us take," says an authority on this subject, "a man with light auburn hair, blue sparkling eyes, a ruddy complexion, ample chest, and muscular, well-rounded, agile frame. When such a man sits down to write, he makes short work of it. He snatches the first pen that comes in the way, never looks how it is pointed, dabs it into the ink, and then dashes on from side to side of the paper in a full, free, and slipshod style, his ideas – or at all events his words – flowing faster than his agile fingers can give them a form.

"On the contrary, select a man with deep black hair, black eyes, brown or sallow complexion, and thin, spare form. After weighing well his subject in his mind, he sits down deliberately, selects and mends his pen, adjusts his paper, and in close, stiff, and upright characters traces at a snail's pace his well-weighed and sententious composition."

NATIONAL DIFFERENCES

Even nations are distinguished by their writing – the vivacity and variableness of the Frenchman, and the delicacy and suppleness of the Italian, are perceptibly distinct from the slowness and strength of the pen discoverable in the phlegmatic German, Dane, and Swede.

THE LEADING CHARACTERISTIC

The characteristic that is most sure to come out in handwriting is individuality. A remarkable man or woman – one with a distinct personality – very seldom writes a quite commonplace hand, and conversely a very distinctive handwriting is generally an index to something distinctive in the character. This is the quality in handwriting that strikes us usually at first sight.

For example:

Approbativeness

Cautiousness

Benevolence

DISTINCT AND CLEAR WRITING ⋇

When the writing is distinct and clear, with short-tailed letters and few dashes, the writer is quiet, sincere, and truthful, with a strong inclination to religion.

A FINE RUNNING HAND ⋇

In a fine running hand, the letters having long tails and curved endings, we see a character enthusiastic and witty. If there are many dashes the writer is as a rule selfish, and we expect to find him or her talkative.

BOLD HANDWRITING

Bold handwriting shows candour and generosity, but at the same time usually indicates a want of tact and sympathy. Should the letters of a bold hand be twisted and marked by flourishes we may infer a hasty temper.

STIFF WRITING

Stiff writing is a sign of reserve, and is often the characteristic of those who are marked by their double cunning. When the up-strokes are thin and broken the writer is of a nervous temperament.

BOLD CAPITALS

Bold capitals indicate pride, united often with a passionate though generous disposition.

UPRIGHT WRITING

When the handwriting is upright and almost perpendicular we may infer love of study and a mind taken up with noble thoughts. If there are no flourishes it shows a fondness for solitude, but an upright hand running into many flourishes is a sign of a social disposition.

INDISTINCT AND CROWDED

When the handwriting is indistinct and the letters are crowded together suspect an uncertain temper, a readiness to take offence at nothing, and a reluctance to make peace after a quarrel.

REGULAR AND WITHOUT FLOURISHES

Writing of great regularity with no flourishes goes with a strong mind, characterised by common sense and mechanical taste.

FLOURISHES AND DASHES

Handwriting with many flourishes and dashes indicates a love of display; in most cases, too, it points to a hasty temper.

SPRAWLING WRITING

Sprawling writing shows an untidy character. We may also infer extravagance and a decidedly frivolous turn, united with a love of fine fashions, but the taste in dress will be bad.

DELICATE HANDWRITING

In the case of even, delicate handwriting, we usually find the sense of time well developed. The habits are also methodical, and the writer will be fond of children.

ECCENTRIC HANDWRITING

Eccentric handwriting does not necessarily impress us with a sense of personality; nor, again, does eccentricity of character at all certainly betray itself in eccentricity of handwriting.

A SMALL, CRAMPED HAND

If the writing is small and cramped, the ends of the words being made straight, then the writer is probably mean in financial affairs, reserved, obstinate, and narrow-minded. When there is a flourish at the ends of the words a hasty temper is to be looked for.

CHAPTER SEVEN

THE
INTERPRETATION
OF YOUR DREAMS

WE TELL THE MEANING
✦ OF YOUR DREAMS ✦

THE oldest dreams on record are those of sacred history, and it is clear from the Bible that dreams are often made use of as a means of revealing things to men, of conveying warnings to them and of lifting the veil that hides from them the future. We must lay ourselves open to receive impressions and have our minds less harassed and obscured than they usually are by the worries of the world if we are to appreciate dreams at their true value and see what a wealth of meaning they sometimes contain.

There are a few points to be kept in mind by all who wish to have a correct understanding of this important subject –

✦ Morning dreams are more reliable than those of any other time, and of morning dreams those of the morning twilight are most valued.

✦ A Friday's dream is the most important dream of the week –

"Friday night's dream
On a Saturday told
Is sure to come true
Be it never so old."

✦ A dream – even a Friday's dream – is only to be absolutely relied upon if repeated three times. It must also be pointed out that there are some dreams as false as can be,

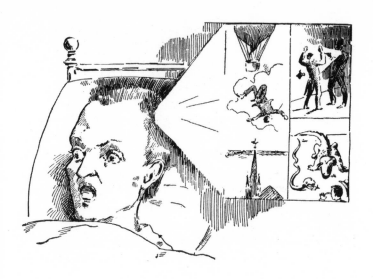

put into people's heads by humorous or ill-disposed spirits. Fun and malice are by no means confined to our little corner of the universe.

In the following pages we have given the meaning of a considerable number of dreams. Once the fundamental principles are grasped, interpretation is easy. Giving all dreams was out of the question, for the land of dreams is as extensive a territory as our waking world.

⁂ ABSENCE

To dream of grieving over the absence of any one is a sure sign that the person dreamt of will soon return. To dream, however, of rejoicing at any one's absence denotes that you will shortly receive intelligence you would rather be without.

✦ ACCOUNTS

If a young woman dreams of an account, or of a bundle of accounts, or of a number of account books, it indicates that she will shortly begin preparations for entering on matrimonial life. When a man dreams of account books it means acquaintance in business with the fickleness of fortune.

✦ ACTOR

To dream of an actor means, in the case of a young woman, that a great deal of the admiration at present paid to her, and which she thinks genuine, is only make-believe.

✦ ACTRESS

To dream of seeing an actress on the stage signifies that you will shortly get into many difficulties, partly through your own indiscretion, and partly from causes over which you have no control. Meeting her in private life in a dream indicates that you are about to discover how "hand in hand with sorrow love is wont to go."

ANTS

To dream of watching ants at work indicates for a young man that he will for a time try to find pleasure in an idle and single life, but that he will at last discover that the truest happiness lies in hard work for the sake of wife and children. The same dream occurring to a young woman foretells that she will soon leave her present ornamental existence to find occupation in rocking the cradle, superintending the meals, and arranging the furniture of the home of somebody.

APRIL FOOL

When a young woman dreams of being made an April Fool, it means that, after having arrived at considerable culture, she will marry one who is a Philistine, and so be exposed to unintelligent criticism and interference. A man dreaming of being made an April Fool may anticipate falling a victim to the false pretences of one in whom he is at present confiding, and may reasonably infer that his only safeguard is a little healthy suspicion.

BALL

Dreams of being at balls and dances and such like festivities are of good omen for lovers –

> "Who dream of being at a ball
> No cause have they for fear,
> For soon they will united be
> To those they hold most dear."

❋ BEES

To dream of bees means general good fortune –
"Happy the man who dreaming sees
The little humble busy bees
Fly humming round their hive."

❋ BICYCLE

To dream of riding on a bicycle means that for some years you will have constant change, always seeking for rest and comfort, but only finding turmoil and disquiet.

❋ BONFIRE

To dream of assisting in making a bonfire indicates that you are on the eve of changing your mind about many things, when you will burn much that you used to worship, and worship much that you used to burn.

❋ BONNET

For a young woman to dream about wearing a new bonnet is a sign that she is about to land in a difficulty through love of finery, desire for admiration and envy of the fine feathers of some of her friends. A young man dreaming of a girl s bonnet, either in a shop window or on her head, may infer that he will enter the matrimonial state before many months have passed.

❋ BOOKSELLER

To dream of meeting a young lady in a bookseller's shop signifies, in the case of a young man, that though he is fond of books he will marry a wife who will care so little for them that when in after life he buys a new book he will carry it home in his hat and creep into the house by the window.

❧ CAGE

To dream of seeing a bird in a cage is a sure sign that you will make a happy marriage and live in harmony so absolute with the object of your choice that you will be independent of the world outside.

❧ CAT

To dream of cats, either in the singular or plural, means that you are about to suffer from the treachery of one in whom you have long trusted. The cats in this case must appear to be alive and active.

❧ CHAIN

To dream of a chain with long links of which you see both the beginning and the end foretells that you will carry on a long correspondence with a certain person, beginning formally and working up to My Dearest So-and-so, but that it will come at last to a cold Sir and Madame, and that will be the end of it.

❧ CLOUD

To dream of a cloud coming for a short while over the sun denotes, should the dreamer be a young man, that the friends of a lady to whom he is attached will place barriers in the way of his intercourse with her, and for a time these will seem insurmountable, but that the tide of fortune will at last begin to flow in his favour, and that he will be received with the heartiest of welcomes by those who formerly would have nothing to say to him. A similar dream in the case of a young woman has much the same signification, but with the sexes reversed.

❧ COOKING CLASS

For a young man to dream that the girl he is paying attention to has begun to attend a cooking class is a sign that should he marry her there is a great probability that she would neglect him and allow his dinner to burn, spending her time in reading novels instead of preparing it properly.

❧ DAGGER

To dream of seeing a dagger, either in the hand of yourself or of any other person, portends that you are about to have a serious argument with an intimate acquaintance, which will end in your becoming enemies for life.

❧ DEAD

To dream of seeing the dead, whether relations or friends, means long life to the living, combined with good health and easy circumstances.

❧ DUNGEON

A dream of being the inmate of a dungeon denotes that in undertaking your present employment you have forged fetters for yourself from which it will take much strength of will to break loose.

❧ DUST

For a girl to dream of being in a dusty house signifies that she will soon be called to keep in order the home of one to whom she has given her heart. A young man, however, dreaming of dusty surroundings is thereby warned that he is in danger of contracting a life-long alliance with a girl who looks too much in the glass ever to be a good housekeeper.

EAR

Dreaming of having a pain in one of your ears is a sure sign that you are about to be made the subject of a false charge, your innocence of which it will be exceedingly difficult to prove.

EYESIGHT

Dreaming of failing eyesight means that you are in danger of wasting your best years and your choicest thoughts on one who is quite unworthy of you.

FIREWORKS

To dream of taking part in an exhibition of fireworks denotes that before long you will be in great danger of losing your temper under the provocations of an acquaintance, and that you will be tempted to commit a personal assault by way of easing and relieving your mind.

FOX

To dream of a fox is for a young woman a dream of warning, intimating that she must not trust to many promises that are now being made to her, because they are insincere.

GAS

To dream of an escape of gas means for a young man that he is on the eve of telling a girl that whilst he is in the world no ill can befall her, but that he will have quarrelled with her and be out of that long promise in a week. For a girl to dream of an escape of gas signifies that her too light-hearted behaviour will in the end so excite the fears of her present sensible lover that he will leave her for ever.

⌇ FLYING

To dream of flying means that you are destined to succeed in high things, and that every obstacle will with you be found to give way before courage and perseverance.

GOLD

To dream of gold signifies that you will be surrounded at last by great magnificence, which you will be unable to enjoy because of disappointment and sickness of heart.

GOOSE

A young man dreaming that he listens to a goose cackling is thereby informed that he is about to write a letter to a young lady, which he will think the cleverest letter he ever wrote in his life, and that the result will fully justify his good opinion of it. A young woman dreaming of a goose may expect to make a fortunate, though not a brilliant, marriage.

GOOSEBERRY

To dream of a gooseberry is, to the lover, of evil import. It means that a friend whom he has introduced to the young woman with whom he is in love will endeavour to supplant him in her good graces, and, what is more, will succeed.

GROPING

To dream that you are groping your way in the dark means that you and the one you have chosen for your life's partner are not at all made for each other, and that after marriage you are certain to have continual friction.

GUITAR

To dream of playing on the guitar, or of hearing it played, is for a young man a sign that his thoughts will or many a day be monopolised by, to him, the dearest and sweetest and best, and that his wooing will be followed by a happy and every way prosperous marriage. A young woman dreaming of guitar playing may also infer from it successful wedlock.

✺ HOTEL

To dream of living in a hotel signifies that you will shortly be compelled by an accident to reside for a time in a hotel in a strange town, and that you will end in marrying the best girl in all that neighbourhood. This is in the case of a man's dreaming. A girl dreaming of hotel life may conclude that she will marry a husband who will be of a roving disposition.

✺ HUNGER

To have hunger enter into a dream is not a good omen, and means that you will be tempted to marry before you have enough for the housekeeping.

✺ ICE

To dream of being on the ice signifies losses of various kinds, especially of money. For a man to dream of ice melting signifies that he will conceive an undying passion for a young woman, and that it will last not longer than fourteen days.

✺ IVY

Dreaming of ivy means to either man or woman that the present engrossing object of affection will soon have to take a back seat, and that one will appear on the scene to whom vows will be paid that are to be really lasting.

⤳ JOURNEY

To dream of going on a journey – whether by rail, coach, carriage, cycle, steamboat, or sailing ship, does not make any difference – means that you are about to have a change in your circumstances.

⤳ JEWEL

To dream of looking at, but not possessing, a rare jewel means that you will shortly meet one whose worth you will at the moment fail to recognise, and whose friendship you will reject, and that that rejected friendship can never afterwards be yours.

⤳ KISSING

To dream of kissing may be pleasant enough while it lasts, but it indicates that in waking hours there will be strife, and that words will run more or less high in proportion to the warmth and enthusiasm recognised in the dream.

⤳ KNIFE

To dream of receiving the present of a knife is a bad omen, for it signifies that many ties in which you take pleasure are about to be cut, and that death and indifference and misunderstanding are about to make sad havoc in the circle of your friends.

⋙ LETTER

To dream of receiving and reading a letter means that you are at present in doubt as to what course of conduct to follow, and that the first words spoken by the first person you meet on the following morning will indicate what you should do.

LADDER

To ascend a ladder in a dream prognosticates your success in the world, but shows that it will not be rapid, for you will go up the ladder of fortune only step by step.

LIBRARY

To dream of being seated in a library means that you have abilities which, rightly cultivated, would enable you to attain to literary distinction.

LILY

For lovers to dream of the lily is good luck. It signifies that all will go well in their happy intercourse, and that their marriage will be crowned with a healthy and remarkably good-looking family.

LION

To dream of meeting a lion indicates that you are about to have some strange adventures, the recounting of which in after life will give great amusement both to yourself and your friends.

MADNESS

To dream of madness in any form is extremely fortunate, indicating that all your undertakings, however unpromising, and perhaps even foolish they may at times appear, will in the end bring success to yourself, and command admiration from your friends.

MALICE

It is well to dream of any one bearing malice towards you, it being a sign that that particular person entertains the most kindly feelings, and would do you a good turn if ever it lay in his or her power.

MAN

For a young woman to dream of talking confidentially to a young man is a happy sign in love affairs. It is all the more promising if he appears in the form of a handsome youth with soft eyes and a settled melancholy expression. For a man to dream of talking to a man foreshadows rivalry in business or in love-making, perhaps in both.

MIRROR

For a girl to dream of a mirror is a sign that she is in danger through studying her looking-glass of neglecting her intellect. It is ominous of future unhappiness, especially if dreamed on a Sunday.

MONEY

Dreams of money are in general unlucky, and point to approaching losses. To dream of finding money is to be dreaded, as to find in a dream is certainly to lose in reality.

MOON

To dream of the moon denotes general good luck. If it sets in a dream it indicates a tranquil, happy existence; if it rises you may expect at a friend's house to meet one who will have a great influence over your destiny.

NECKLACE

To dream of wearing a costly necklace is for a woman an unfortunate sign, denoting that she will probably have more splendour than happiness in her wedded life.

NEWSPAPER

Reading a newspaper in a dream indicates that an expected note is sure to arrive, though its contents will hardly be to your liking.

NOSE

To dream of any one having a long nose means the coming of death, and *the longer the nose the more speedy the end*.

OAK

To dream of an oak means that you will have a long life, and remarkable health and strength as well.

✦ OCEAN

Should you see the ocean in a dream, and its surface be calm, you may infer that your circumstances for the present will continue without change or disturbance, but should the sea be stormy it is proper to expect that your life will shortly become unsettled.

✦ OIL

To dream of oil or of its use means that you will be shortly in danger of getting into trouble through a too free use of your tongue.

✦ OWL

To dream of an owl is an unlucky incident. For the young it predicts that they are in danger of forming a matrimonial alliance with those who are heavy and stupid. For the middle-aged and old it denotes the approach of poverty.

❧ PAINTING

To dream of painting – whether it be the walls of your house or a palace or anything else – is a good sign, meaning that what mistakes you have committed in the earlier part of your life will all be forgotten, and that you will come to occupy an honourable position in the world.

❊ PEACOCK

To dream of seeing a peacock means for a young woman that she is shortly to marry a man of good looks but with brains badly placed; and for a man it signifies that he is to marry a young woman with the same characteristics.

❊ PEARLS

There is great good luck in dreaming of pearls. For a young woman it signifies that she is destined to marry one who will not only prove an affectionate husband, but will be able to supply her with all the pleasures and luxuries that riches can command. A man dreaming of pearls thereby learns the fact that he will marry for love, and that after his marriage great riches will come to him through his wife.

❊ PIES

To dream of watching a woman making pies means that your experience in love is likely to prove disastrous, and that you may come in the end to have as many wounds in your heart as there will be wrinkles on your face. Dreaming of eating pies – whether they be meat pies or fruit pies, it is all one – signifies that you will shortly have an opportunity of laughing at something till your head aches.

POETRY

To dream of writing verses and having a young lady criticise them denotes that you are never likely to marry, even though you fall in love countless times and write poetry about all your objects of affection.

QUARREL

Taking part in a quarrel in a dream is not good luck, and foretells that you may expect soon to be an unwilling listener to a conversation in which you will hear no good of yourself.

QUEEN

To dream of seeing the Queen means for a man that he will shortly marry a woman who will so rule his house that without her permission he will not get so much as a lump of sugar.

✤ RIBBON

For a young woman to dream of ribbons is a sign that she is about to have a new beau, who will pay her many embarrassing attentions, but after fluttering round her for a short time will leave her for one with the reputation of possessing considerable means.

✤ RIVAL

To dream of the discovery of a rival is one of the best omens in love affairs. It means that you will shortly be united to the object of your affections, and that few anywhere in after life will be happier than you two.

✤ RIVER

A dream by a man of sailing up or down a river denotes that he will shortly be wedded to one of an imperious disposition, and that in after life, according to her will, so must be everything.

✤ ROPE

It is a bad sign to dream of a rope. You may infer from it that you are in danger of being bound in fetters, willingly no doubt at first, but from which you will ere long desire hopelessly to get free.

✤ SALMON

A dream in which salmon play a prominent part, whether in being caught or eaten, denotes that you are likely to see much of the world before being at last fettered by the chains of wedlock.

SEWING

For a young woman to dream of sewing is a favourable omen, indicating that she will shortly be united to one of the most loving of husbands, whose home she will make happy and comfortable by her good sense and industry.

SHIPWRECK

To dream of a voyage in which you are shipwrecked means that you and a companion will shortly start on a journey with much mutual affection, but that you will return hating each other with intense animosity.

SHOOTING STAR

To dream of seeing a shooting star has for lovers this meaning, that their affection will be so ardent that kisses thick and innumerable will be given and taken on both sides.

❧ SLIPPERS

For a bachelor to dream of a pair of slippers portends his speedy marriage; for a young woman it signifies that she has recently met him who in all probability will be her partner for life.

❧ TELEGRAM

For a young woman to dream of receiving or sending a telegram means that she is about to form a friendship with a young man so close and intimate that all their friends and enemies will be in common. And this friendship will ripen at last into love, and be crowned by a happy marriage.

❧ THEATRE

To dream of being in the theatre means that the realities of life will soon cease to interest you, that you will take refuge in Dreamland, and live on illusions till your last hour.

❧ TUNNEL

To dream of going through a tunnel with a light at the end is a good dream for the depressed, for it signifies that if their lives are now dull and gloomy they will brighten up in the long run into peace and joy.

VISIT

To dream of receiving a visit means that you ought to cultivate the art of being friendly with all you meet, because a stranger will shortly be introduced to you who will have it in his power to make your fortune.

WOMAN

A dream in which an old woman figures largely is of happy import. It means safety, prosperity, and comfort. To dream of a young woman means much the same thing, but these good features will be combined with not a few worries and distractions.

YORKSHIRE PUDDING

To dream of eating Yorkshire pudding means for a young man that, though at present much taken up with the idea of good living – substantial dinners and the like – he is shortly to meet one who will alter the current of his thoughts and convince him that it is love after all that makes the world go round.

YOUTH

For a girl to dream of seeing a handsome but unknown youth means that she is about to transfer her affections from one with whom she at present thinks she is in love and give them to another, and that her present love compared with her future passion will be as a farthing cracker is to a volcano.